continental
café

recipes to eat
at home

carolyn humphries

foulsham

LONDON • NEW YORK • TORONTO • SYDNEY

foulsham

The Publishing House, Bennetts Close, Cippenham,
Slough, Berkshire, SL1 5AP, England

ISBN 0-572-02908-X

Cover and inside photographs by Carol and Terry Pastor

A CIP record for this book is available from the British Library.

With thanks to the following companies for providing items for the photographs. The blue mussel bowl
(photograph opposite page 24): Campbell and Brown, Country Style for Your House and Garden, 66a St John's Street,
Bury St Edmunds, Suffolk, IP33 1SJ. Tablecloth (photograph opposite page 49): HAGA (Home and Garden Accessories),
Contemporary Homewares and Furnishings, 12 St John Street, Bury St Edmunds, Suffolk, IP33 1SQ
(e-mail: jeri@hagauk.com).

Printed in Great Britain by St Edmundsbury Press, Bury St Edmunds, Suffolk

Contents

Introduction

Most people associate continental café-style cooking with France. But it has become much more than the cuisine of one single country. It is an eclectic mix of styles, that uses all the influences and favourite regional dishes from all over Europe, blending them to create imaginative masterpieces that amalgamate the best of culture, taste and texture. It merges tradition with innovation, creating explosions of colour and flavour that delight the eye and excite the taste buds.

This book brings together a fabulous collection of recipes, so that you can introduce that style and flavour right into your home. You'll find all the classics, each with a clever serving suggestion or neat personal twist, plus a whole raft of new ideas. But they all share that wonderful, relaxed and delicious touch that is true café style.

When you are planning your meal, just browse through the recipes and imagine that you are looking at your favourite café menu, first choosing the main dish you fancy, then the starter and dessert that will complement it perfectly. There's plenty of choice: soups, appetisers, seafood, vegetarian and meat main courses, pasta and pizzas, rice and salads, and – for many people the most popular of all – a mouth-watering dessert menu. I've also put together a range of cocktails and speciality coffees, so you can set the scene and follow your theme right through to the end of the party.

All the recipes are arranged step by step so they are easy to follow, whatever your culinary skills may be. Don't be put off if some of them look rather long: each main course dish is presented with built-in accompaniments, so you won't have to hunt through the book for a suitable sauce or side dish – everything you need to create the whole course is all there in one place. I've also given you plenty of suitable serving suggestions for each meal, with extra hints and variations that you can try, plus a selection of notes on special ingredients and tips on presentation that will bring real café style to your cooking.

So with my book as a guide, you can start experimenting with this exciting style of cuisine and learn how to create the most wonderful dishes to impress your friends and family. *Bon appétit!*

Café-style Entertaining

When you are entertaining, you want everything, from selecting your menu to presenting the food and pouring the wine, to go off perfectly. Just a little thought and planning will make all the difference to the success of the occasion.

Setting the scene

Café-style entertaining should be high on style and low on stress. Aim to achieve a low-key, relaxed atmosphere.

Soft lighting is essential. Choose table or standard lamps or wall lights rather than a bright central overhead light (unless you have a dimmer switch). But don't have it so dark that your guests can't appreciate the beautiful creations you are serving them! Supplement the lamps with a candle on the table, especially if it's a romantic occasion.

Choose some smooth, downbeat music. You are looking for something that will contribute to the atmosphere but not distract from the conversation or the food, so keep the volume down – it's not called 'background music' for nothing. Soft music will not only keep you relaxed while you prepare the meal, it will also help to break the ice while you and your guests chat and enjoy your pre-dinner drinks, and wait for everyone to arrive before you sit down to eat.

The design of your table setting is important in setting the scene for the meal. You should try to create an informal look, but do avoid a red checked cloth and a candle in a Chianti bottle – they're decidedly passé! That said, simplicity is important, so this is not an occasion for the candelabra and the polished silverware. Instead, if you've got a decent wooden table, all you need to do is put out your place mats, or perhaps a plain coloured cloth. Opt for a single candle and just one flower, or a plain arrangement, rather than a big centrepiece.

Choose plain white crockery if possible. If you don't have white, any plain colour will be effective; busy patterns detract from both the atmosphere and the food. Really large plates are best: when you are serving a café-style meal, large plates allow you to go to town with your presentation and to make the food look more attractive. They also provide more space around the food, so that you can add a drizzle of sauce or a dusting of icing sugar without it smothering the food or crowding the ingredients together. The effect you're looking for is a bit like minimalist room design – white space, clear surfaces, attractive but uncluttered decoration, with clever touches of colour here and there to add contrast.

Linen napkins are best when you are entertaining guests. If you prefer to use disposable napkins, buy large linen-effect paper ones. Either fold them neatly and place them in the glasses or put them on side plates, whichever you prefer. Forget those water-lilies and bishops' hats that we used to put on the place mats – they went out with the candles stuck in the wine bottles.

On a practical note, make sure each guest has enough cutlery for every course – arrange it on either side of the plate (not above the place mat), starting with the first course and working from the outside in. Set out glasses for wine and water, and don't forget the serving spoons and salad servers if you need them.

Choosing your menu

In general, the easiest route to is to select your main course first, then choose some suitable accompaniments (I've done this bit for you!), and finally decide which starter and dessert will make the perfect meal. The key word to remember is variety. You need to consider several different elements, and these apply whether you are eating in a restaurant or choosing dishes to serve at home.

First, you should avoid any repetition of ingredients. For instance, you shouldn't serve a fish soup followed by a fish main course, or a fruit starter followed by a meat and fruit main course and a fruity pudding.

You'll also need to consider the cooking methods. For example, a fried cheese and cranberry starter, followed by deep-fried plaice and oysters, with pancakes for dessert would probably be too much for even the most ardent lover of fried food.

Vary the temperature of the food too, for your own sake as much as your guests'. Don't go for all hot dishes (too much to keep warm) or all cold (not enough variety). If you choose a hot starter and hot main course, always go for a cold dessert. The most practical choice from the cook's point of view is to serve a cold starter and dessert, as they can be made in advance – with just a few last-minute finishing touches, perhaps – with a hot main course.

Try to introduce lots of different colours and textures. The combination of fried foods I mentioned above would be predominantly brown – not a good choice unless you want your meal to look dull and unappetising – and there would be rather too much 'crunch' in the texture. The combinations and presentations of everything in this book have been carefully selected to help you produce dishes that look and taste interesting and exciting!

Choosing the drinks

You will almost certainly be serving aperitifs before the meal. Once again, the best advice here is to keep it simple. If there's too much choice, your guests will take longer to make their decision and settle down to relax – and it's more trouble for you, as well. I like to serve a choice of one or two cocktails, and I've included lots of ideas for these on pages 134–39. Another option is to offer a glass of sparkling wine – either plain or with orange juice (Buck's Fizz) or blackcurrant liqueur (Kir Royale). Alternatively, you can simply offer red or white wine or beer.

Always provide sparkling or still water and other soft drinks, such as pure fruit juices or carbonated drinks, even if you know that no one is driving.

Don't offer huge bowls of nibbles with your pre-dinner drinks – they'll only fill people up. At most, a dish of olives and perhaps some baby gherkins, nuts or some interesting flavoured crisps are sufficient.

When it comes to providing drinks to accompany the meal itself, most people like a choice of red or white wine, and you should always offer water to your guests as well. Strictly speaking, to be true to the style of this book I suppose you should choose French or Italian wines, but I think that's going too far: if you have a favourite, who cares if it's Australian!

For informal, café-style eating, the old rules of white wine with fish and white meat and red wine with red meats and cheese have pretty much gone out of the window. Everything is much more relaxed now and everyone should have what they like best. However, some wines will obviously complement particular ingredients better than others. Hefty, robust wines, whether white – such as heavily oaked Chardonnays – or red – such as Cabernet Sauvignon – will always need a strongly flavoured dish.

In the end, your choice of wine will depend on your own palate and pocket, but try to select wines that you think will go well with the courses you have chosen. Keep the white wines chilled. Most red wines are best at room temperature, although there are a few younger, lighter red wines that benefit from a spell in the fridge.

Presenting the meal

The appearance of a meal will affect your guests' appetites just as much as its smell and taste. It is well worth spending a little extra time on presentation – it will add to the atmosphere and the sight of a meal that looks beautiful will make your guests want to sit down and eat it.

One of the other great things about continental café cuisine is that each course is brought to the table, already on the plates. This is much simpler for everyone – no awkward dishing-up at the table, and no more angst for the poor cook as the lasagne slops all over the tablecloth or the pavlova shatters into a thousand fragments in front of the guests. To achieve this, I have included tips on presentation throughout the book, so that each course will look as well as taste fabulous, giving your family or friends a great gourmet experience. The different elements of each dish are carefully arranged on each guest's plate with a simple but effective garnish, making it a pleasure to look at as well as to eat.

Creating the careless look – carefully

You will have noticed that when you've eaten in cafés, the food has a wonderfully informal look about it. The style is definitely casual, so this is not the place for regimented rows of chopped herbs or swirls of meticulously piped cream. Instead, there will be a few fresh herb leaves, casually tossed over a sauce, or a light dusting of icing sugar over a pudding, and dribbles and crumbs are positively encouraged. It is, of course, carefully contrived –

achieving that haphazard look doesn't happen just by chance – but if overdone, it can look like a dogs' dinner.

Don't be put off, however – there's nothing difficult about it, and you can achieve it quite easily. It's a very good idea to practise first, with some dummy ingredients and a plain plate. When arranging salad, start with a neat pile, then pull a few leaves away from the main bunch, to lie slightly more randomly on the plate. To present a main ingredient, don't set things in neat piles – allow morsels to tumble off. If you're serving a bed of rice, allow a few grains to stray carelessly from the rest. Most importantly, don't overcrowd the plate – the effect should be that there is plenty of space, not a mountain of food.

Sauces are perfect for achieving the look you want. Dribble them sparingly down the sides of things, and let a few drops trickle across the plate. Put only a little on the plate (you can always hand more separately in a jug). Oils and other liquids are good too – you've probably seen chefs on TV with their thumb over the neck of a bottle of oil, vinegar or wine, letting just a thin trickle come out. It's a simple trick, which doesn't take long to master, but you don't want to risk letting lots splash over your finished dish, so do try it out beforehand. If you'd rather not use your thumb, buy specialist oil and vinegar cans or bottles with thin spouts – the results will be the same. Whatever you do, remember 'Less is more'. Aim for trickles and trails, not splashes and mess.

Using colour and shape

Imagine every meal as a picture. You want to achieve mouth-watering combinations of colour as well as texture and flavour. But you don't want to produce something that looks like a rainbow so, once again, go for understated elegance. There is something very inviting about several different subtle shades of green arranged around a piece of meat on a white plate. But do add colour to enhance your meal where necessary. For example, if you are using white plates to serve pale food, a dusting of red paprika could give it a real lift. In the same way, if you are serving seasonal vegetables to accompany your main course, arrange them so that the colours complement each other. Put baby carrots next to mangetout, with new potatoes at one end. Don't sit potatoes next to cauliflower or butter beans – if you must serve them at the same time, make sure there is a colourful alternative – such as green beans or tomatoes – in between.

Think about shapes too: if you are serving green beans, courgettes and carrots, don't cut them all into strips – leave the beans whole, slice the courgettes diagonally and chop the carrots into little dice.

Adding those little extras

Garnishes should be kept simple too – but that doesn't mean they can't be imaginative. Slices and wedges of lemon, sprigs of fresh herbs and finely chopped parsley or coriander will add colour to a dish. But you can go a step further and use edible fresh flowers or flowering herbs. Don't buy them from a florist – they will probably have been treated with pesticides. They are available from large supermarkets or, of course, you could grow your own. Don't use too many – one or two at most, or perhaps just a few petals – and choose small blooms or sprigs. Here's a brief list of some of my favourites for decorating plates and brightening up savoury and sweet dishes and salads: calendula, chrysanthemum (blanch first, then scatter the petals over), daisies, dandelions, geraniums, honeysuckle, marigolds, pansies, roses and violets.

Keeping it hot

One of the biggest problems when dishing up a café-style meal is keeping everything hot while you're arranging it on the plates. The following tips will help:

- Plan exactly what you have to do at the last minute. Write it down if necessary. You won't have time to start referring to the recipes when everything is getting cold.

- Don't attempt to serve a hot starter, main course and dessert – it's impossible to keep that much food hot for six or more people. Serve a mixture of hot and cold dishes.

- Close windows and doors to prevent draughts when serving up. You won't believe how quickly food cools when that north wind blows through the kitchen window!

- Make sure all plates for serving hot food are very hot before serving up. If you don't have room to keep them hot, have a bowl of boiling water handy to dip them in, then dry them and use immediately.

- Prepare everything you can in advance and keep warm in a low oven. (There will, of course, be a few foods that can only be prepared at the last minute.)

- Some accompanying vegetables can be cooked in advance, then either reheated quickly in saucepans or zapped in the microwave just before serving.

- Vegetables that only need the shortest of cooking times should be cooked at the last minute while you are serving everything else, then added to the plates.

- Reheat sauces until piping hot before spooning on to plates.

- Have all your garnishes prepared in advance ready to add at the last minute. You don't want to be chopping parsley or peeling fruit when the food is ready and cooling as you work.

- Set everything on a work surface or table large enough to take all the plates side by side. That way you can work along them, in a sort of conveyor belt, arranging the food.

- Make sure you have help to carry the plates to the table. As one plate is finished, it can be taken through as you finish the next one. That way, they will all be served at the earliest possible opportunity.

- Have a new, damp, disposable cloth handy to wipe up unplanned spills on plates (and your fingers) as you arrange the food.

- Keep calm. Don't panic and rush, or it will all go wrong. If you think the food is getting cold, zap each plate in the microwave for just a minute before it's carried through to the table (but remember to leave off any salad or garnish until after it's reheated!)

Notes on the Recipes

- All ingredients are given in imperial, metric and American measures. Follow one set only in a recipe. American terms are given in brackets.
- All spoon measures are level: 1 tsp=5 ml; 1 tbsp=15 ml.
- Eggs are medium unless otherwise stated.
- The ingredients are listed in the order in which they are used in the recipes.
- Always wash, peel, core and seed, if necessary, fresh produce before use.
- Seasoning and the use of strongly flavoured ingredients such as garlic or chillies are very much a matter of personal taste. Adjust to suit your own palate.
- Always use fresh herbs unless dried are specifically called for. If you wish to substitute dried for fresh, use only half the quantity or less, as they are very pungent. Frozen, chopped varieties have a better colour and flavour than dried. Only fresh herbs are suitable for garnishing, although bright green dried parsley flakes can be dusted round a plate.
- All can and packet sizes are approximate as they vary from brand to brand.

- Cooking times are approximate and should be used as a guide only. Always check that food is piping hot and cooked through before serving.
- Always cook on the shelf just above the centre of the oven unless otherwise stated.
- I use butter throughout the book as it gives the best flavour in many dishes. If you are worried about cholesterol or your weight, use a butter-flavoured low-fat spread instead but make sure it is suitable for cooking as well as spreading.
- Many of my recipes call for cream or crème fraîche. You must use full-fat varieties if the dish is boiled – if low-fat creams are brought to boiling point, they will curdle. You may substitute low-fat varieties for cold dishes, garnishes or decorations or any dish that does not require boiling.
- In the desserts, I have often used a vanilla pod infused in milk for flavouring. If you prefer, you can flavour the milk with about 2.5 ml/½ tsp of natural vanilla essence (extract) and omit the heating and infusing before use.
- All the recipes serve six. It is simple, however, to divide the quantities to serve two or four, or increase them to serve eight should the need arise.

Using Olive Oil

Olive oil is widely acknowledged to be the best oil there is for culinary use, and it is an essential ingredient in café-style cuisine. It comes in several different grades. Extra-virgin olive oil comes from the first pressing of the olives and is strictly regulated to ensure that it is of the highest quality, with an acidity of less than 1 per cent. It has a deep colour, ranging from glowing yellowish-green to a dark olive, and a rich, fruity flavour. It is wonderful for dressings and in condiments and is frequently used for dipping bread in, instead of spreading with butter. The flavour varies considerably from one brand to another and preference is a matter of personal taste. Cost is no guide – the most expensive is not always the best, so buy a small bottle first to test.

Virgin olive oil is also from first-pressed olives but has a higher acidity and a slightly less pleasing aroma. It is less expensive, but still of high quality.

Unclassified olive oil is the cheapest and is far less distinctive. It is too bland to be used to make condiments, but it is actually more suitable than its stronger-flavoured counterparts for making things such as mayonnaise.

Olive oil may be used for sautéing but not for deep-frying as it has a lower smoking point than vegetable, nut and seed oils.

Olive oil starts to deteriorate as soon as it is bottled, so it should be stored in a cool dark place (not the fridge) and used within six months of purchase.

stocks

To produce the best meals, you do need to use the best
ingredients, which usually means the freshest. One ingredient
that forms the basis of so many café-style dishes is fresh
stock. No self-respecting café chef would use stock cubes, so
I have devoted this first section to stock recipes alone. You can
store cooked, cooled stocks in the fridge in an airtight
container for three days, or you can freeze them.
If you don't want to make your own, you can use either a
chilled stock from the supermarket, or a bouillon powder or
cube with water, but always buy the best-quality you can find,
and don't make the stock too strong or you'll smother rather
than enhance the flavour of the dish.

Simple fish stock

If you aren't using the trimmings from a whole fish that you are cooking yourself, ask your fishmonger for some. You can use any kind of fish to make a stock and you can vary the vegetables and herbs according to what you have to hand.

MAKES ABOUT 1 LITRE/1¾ PTS/4¼ CUPS

1 kg/2¼ lb fish trimmings, e.g. heads, tails, bones, skin

1 onion, roughly chopped

1 carrot, roughly chopped

2 celery sticks, roughly cut up

1 bouquet garni sachet

6 black peppercorns

1 litre/1¾ pts/4¼ cups water

150 ml/¼ pt/⅔ cup white wine or cider

2.5 ml/½ tsp salt

1 Put all the ingredients into a large saucepan.

2 Bring to the boil, then reduce the heat, part-cover and simmer gently for 40 minutes.

3 Strain through a very fine sieve (strainer).

4 Cover, leave to cool, then chill. Use as required.

Hints and variations All stocks can be stored in the fridge in an airtight container for up to three days. Alternatively, you can divide up what you don't need immediately into small, measured portions and freeze for up to three months.

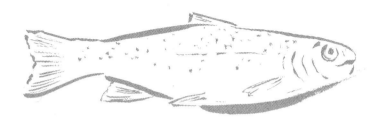

Vegetable stock

Vegetable stock is much quicker to make than meat stock, as the flavour is quickly extracted from the vegetables. As with other stocks, you can adjust the ingredients and the quantities to suit what you have available.

MAKES ABOUT 1.2 LITRES/2 PTS/5 CUPS

I large onion, roughly chopped

1 large carrot, roughly chopped

2 celery sticks, roughly chopped

1 small turnip, roughly chopped

1 large leek, roughly chopped

1.5 litres/2½ pts/6 cups water

1 bouquet garni sachet

2.5 ml/½ tsp salt

Plenty of freshly ground black pepper

1 Put all the ingredients in a large saucepan.

2 Bring to the boil and skim the surface. Reduce the heat, cover and simmer very gently for 45 minutes.

3 Strain the stock through a fine sieve (strainer) into a bowl.

4 Cover, leave to cool, then chill. Use as required.

Hints and variations If you have a pressure cooker, you can make the stocks in half the time. Follow the manufacturer's guide for times.

White chicken stock

If you can't get a boiling fowl, buy the cheapest small chicken you can find.
Thaw it, if frozen, before cooking. After boiling, the meat can be picked off and used
for any recipe calling for cooked chicken.

MAKES ABOUT 1.2 LITRES/2 PTS/5 CUPS

1 boiling fowl or small chicken

2 litres/3½ pts/8½ cups water

1 celery stick, chopped

1 onion, quartered

1 leek, white part only, chopped

1 bouquet garni sachet

Salt and freshly ground black pepper

1 Put the boiling fowl or chicken in a saucepan and cover with cold water. Add the remaining ingredients.

2 Bring to the boil, skim the surface, then reduce the heat, cover and simmer gently for 2–2½ hours. Use a draining spoon to remove any scum from the surface several times during cooking.

3 Strain the contents of the pan through a sieve (strainer) into a bowl. Leave until it stops dripping. Taste the stock and re-season, if necessary.

4 Cover, leave to cool, then chill. Skim off any fat and use as required.

Chicken carcass stock

The carcass of a cooked chicken is full of goodness and flavour, so don't
throw it away when you've made a roast dinner – it can be used to make this
delicious stock.

MAKES ABOUT 900 ML/1½ PTS/3¾ CUPS

1 cooked chicken carcass

1 onion

1 bay leaf

1 carrot, cut into chunks

Salt and freshly ground black pepper

1 Break up the carcass and put it in a saucepan with the onion, bay leaf and carrot. Add a little salt and pepper. Cover with water.

2 Bring to the boil, cover, then reduce the heat and simmer very gently for 2 hours.

3 Strain the stock through a sieve (strainer) into a bowl.

4 Cover, leave to cool, then chill. Use as required.

Brown meat stock

Browning the meat and vegetables in the oven gives a good meat stock more flavour and colour, which it will then impart to the dish you are making. You can use other vegetables, such as swede or turnip, if you like.

MAKES ABOUT 900 ML/1½ PTS/3¾ CUPS

2 onions, roughly chopped

1 large carrot, roughly chopped

1 celery stick, roughly chopped

225 g/8 oz stewing beef, diced

450 g/1 lb beef (or other meat) bones

1 bouquet garni sachet

2.5 ml/½ tsp Worcestershire sauce

2 litres/3½ pts/8½ cups water

2.5 ml/½ tsp salt

Plenty of freshly ground black pepper

1 Preheat the oven to 220°C/425°F/gas 7/fan oven 200°C.

2 Spread the vegetables out in a roasting tin (pan) and arrange the meat and bones on top. Roast in the oven for 40 minutes.

3 Tip the contents of the pan into a large saucepan and add the remaining ingredients.

4 Bring to the boil and skim the surface with a draining spoon. Turn down the heat, cover and simmer very gently for 4 hours.

5 Strain through a fine sieve (strainer) into a bowl.

6 Cover, leave to cool, then chill. Remove any fat from the surface before using as required.

soups and appetisers

The first course you put on the table will set the scene for what is to come. Presentation is all-important to tempt your guests' taste buds, so make good use of fresh ingredients and colourful garnishes. Keep the portion sizes small – you want to whet everyone's appetite, not dull it completely.

When making soup, for best results, use home-made stock (see pages 10–14). If you don't have the time, buy good-quality chilled stock or the best-quality stock cubes.

Provençal vegetable soup
with Camargue red rice

A selection of Mediterranean vegetables simmered with red rice and flavoured with oregano and a hint of garlic, finished with a scattering of fresh basil and grated hard goats' cheese.

SERVES 6

15 ml/1 tbsp olive oil

1 onion, finely chopped

1 garlic clove, crushed

1 green (bell) pepper, finely chopped

1 red pepper, finely chopped

1 large courgette (zucchini),
finely chopped

1 small aubergine (eggplant),
finely chopped

400 g/14 oz/1 large can of
chopped tomatoes

30 ml/2 tbsp tomato purée (paste)

1 litre/1¾ pts/4¼ cups chicken or
vegetable stock

2.5 ml/½ tsp dried oregano

5 ml/1 tsp caster (superfine) sugar

Salt and freshly ground black pepper

50 g/2 oz/¼ cup Camargue red rice

15 ml/1 tbsp chopped fresh basil

50 g/2 oz/½ cup finely grated
hard goats' cheese

1 Heat the oil in a large saucepan and fry (sauté) the onion and garlic for 2 minutes, stirring until softened but not browned.

2 Add all the remaining ingredients except the basil and cheese.

3 Bring to the boil, reduce the heat, part-cover and simmer gently for 20 minutes until the vegetables and rice are tender. Taste and re-season, if necessary.

4 Ladle into warm, wide, shallow soup bowls, sprinkle with the basil and cheese and serve hot.

Serving suggestions Hot French bread is the best accompaniment.

Hints and variations If you use soup pasta instead of rice, and Parmesan instead of the goats' cheese, you've created an Italian minestra instead of a French potage. Serve it with warm ciabatta bread.

Café style Camargue red rice, a variety that comes from the wetlands of Southern France, adds an unusual touch to this dish. It has a wonderful deep red colour and distinctive, nutty flavour.

French red onion soup
with Gruyère croûtes

Caramelised red onions, cooked gently in a good vegetable stock to create a rich flavoursome soup, served with toasted slices of French bread smothered in melting, port-laced Gruyère, floating on top.

SERVES 6

15 ml/1 tbsp olive oil

15 g/½ oz/1 tbsp butter

450 g/1 lb red onions, halved and thinly sliced

15 g/½ oz/1 tbsp demerara sugar

1.2 litres/2 pts/5 cups vegetable stock

Salt and freshly ground black pepper

FOR THE CROÛTES

100 g/4 oz/1 cup finely grated Gruyère (Swiss) cheese

10 g/2 tsp butter

30 ml/2 tbsp port

6 slices of French bread

1 Heat the oil and butter in a large saucepan. Add the onions and fry (sauté), stirring, over a moderate heat for 5 minutes until lightly golden.

2 Add the sugar and continue to cook for a further 2–3 minutes until richly caramelised (take care not to let them burn).

3 Add the stock, bring back to the boil, reduce the heat and simmer for 15 minutes. Season to taste with salt and pepper.

4 Meanwhile, mash the cheese with the butter and the port until blended.

5 Toast the bread on both sides. Pile the cheese on the slices, pressing firmly.

6 Ladle the soup into warm flameproof bowls. Float a piece of the cheese toast on top of each and place under a preheated grill (broiler) for about 3 minutes until the cheese melts and bubbles. Serve straight away.

Hints and variations You can make a traditional French onion soup by using ordinary onions and meat stock. Top the French bread with plain Gruyère instead of the cheese and port mixture.

Salmon bisque

with white wine and cream

Fresh salmon simmered in a tomato and white wine stock, delicately flavoured with leeks, then puréed until smooth, thickened with potato and finished with cream and a touch of brandy for added sophistication.

SERVES 6

1 leek, finely chopped

15 g/½ oz/1 tbsp butter

1 large potato, diced

225 g/8 oz salmon steak, skinned

450 ml/¾ pt/2 cups fish stock

300 ml/½ pt/1¼ cups dry white wine

1 bouquet garni sachet

1 large tomato, skinned, seeded and finely chopped

Salt and freshly ground black pepper

15 ml/1 tbsp brandy

150 ml/¼ pt/⅔ cup milk

90 ml/6 tbsp single (light) cream

30 ml/2 tbsp chopped fresh parsley, for garnishing

1 In a large saucepan, fry (sauté) the leek in the butter for 2 minutes, stirring, until softened but not browned.

2 Stir in the potato and cook gently for 30 seconds.

3 Add the fish, stock, wine, bouquet garni and tomato. Season lightly. Bring to the boil, reduce the heat, part-cover and simmer very gently for 20 minutes until the potatoes and fish are tender.

4 Carefully lift the fish out of the pan with a draining spoon. Remove any bones and discard. Discard the bouquet garni.

5 Put the fish in a blender or food processor with the remaining contents of the pan and purée until smooth.

6 Return to the saucepan. Stir in the brandy, milk and cream and season to taste. Reheat but do not boil. Ladle into warm bowls and garnish with chopped parsley before serving.

Serving suggestions I like to serve warmed tiny granary rolls with this soup.

Fresh tomato soup

with vodka

Crushed ripe plum tomatoes simmered with celery, shallots and vegetable stock, a shot of vodka to give an added kick, and finished with crème fraîche and snipped fresh chives.

SERVES 6

15 g/½ oz/1 tbsp butter

15 ml/1 tbsp olive oil

3 shallots, roughly chopped

2 celery sticks, sliced

700 g/1½ lb fresh plum tomatoes, skinned and roughly chopped

600 ml/1 pt/2½ cups vegetable stock

30 ml/2 tbsp tomato purée (paste)

5 ml/1 tsp caster (superfine) sugar

2.5 ml/½ tsp dried basil

Salt and freshly ground black pepper

90 ml/6 tbsp vodka

45 ml/3 tbsp crème fraîche

15 ml/1 tbsp snipped fresh chives

6 small inner celery sticks, with leaves, for garnishing

1 Heat the butter and oil and fry (sauté) the shallots and celery for 2 minutes, stirring, until softened but not browned.

2 Add the tomatoes, stock, tomato purée, sugar and basil and season with a little salt and pepper.

3 Bring to the boil, part-cover, reduce the heat and simmer gently for 20 minutes.

4 Purée in a blender or food processor, then strain through a fine sieve (strainer) back into the pan.

5 Add the vodka and reheat but do not boil. Taste and re-season, if necessary.

6 Ladle into deep soup cups. Add a spoonful of crème fraîche to each and sprinkle with the chives. Stand a celery stick in each cup and serve straight away.

Serving suggestions Cheese straws or wafers make a delicious accompaniment.

Hints and variations To peel tomatoes, place them in a large bowl, cover with boiling water and leave to stand for 30 seconds. Then drain in a colander and rinse with cold water. The skins will now peel off easily. For speed, you can use two 400 g/14 oz/large cans of peeled plum tomatoes, but the flavour won't be as good. The soup is also delicious chilled before serving.

SOUPS AND APPETISERS

Minted green pea soup
with crispy bacon

A brightly coloured but delicately flavoured soup, enriched with a little crème fraîche and topped with a spoonful of crisp, crumbled smoked bacon to give a lovely contrast of texture and flavour.

SERVES 6

25 g/1 oz/2 tbsp butter

1 bunch of spring onions (scallions), roughly chopped

1 potato, peeled and diced

450 g/1 lb frozen peas

1 large sprig of fresh mint

1.2 litres/2 pts/5 cups vegetable stock

5 ml/1 tsp caster (superfine) sugar

Salt and freshly ground black pepper

60 ml/4 tbsp crème fraîche

4 rashers (slices) of smoked streaky bacon, rinded

6 tiny sprigs of fresh mint, for garnishing

1 Melt the butter in a large pan and fry (sauté) the spring onions for 2 minutes, stirring, until softened but not browned.

2 Add the potato, peas, mint, stock, sugar and a little salt and pepper and bring to the boil. Part-cover, reduce the heat and simmer gently for 20 minutes. Discard the sprig of mint.

3 Purée the soup in a blender or food processor. Pass it through a fine sieve (strainer), to remove the pea skins, and return to the pan. Stir in the crème fraîche, taste and re-season, if necessary.

4 Meanwhile, grill (broil) or dry-fry the bacon until crisp, turning once. Drain on kitchen paper (paper towels). Either snip with scissors or crumble into small pieces.

5 Ladle the soup into warm soup cups, sprinkle a little bacon in the centre and add a small sprig of fresh mint. Serve straight away.

Serving suggestions For added impact, blanch 12 mangetout (snow peas) for 1 minute in boiling water. Drain, rinse with cold water and drain again. Split each mangetout along one edge and fill with chive-flavoured soft cheese (you'll need about 50 g/2 oz/¼ cup in all). Serve the soup in soup cups standing on small plates and arrange two of the stuffed mangetout beside the soup cup on each plate, garnished with a tiny sprig of parsley.

Sweet potato and coriander soup
with olive croûtons

A smooth, puréed soup flavoured with coriander and enriched with egg yolk and cream, scattered with crisp, golden cubes of fried bread, sandwiched with black and green olives.

SERVES 6

25 g/1 oz/2 tbsp unsalted (sweet) butter

1 bunch of spring onions (scallions), chopped

1 large sweet potato, diced

1 large floury potato, diced

2.5 ml/½ tsp ground coriander (cilantro)

1.2 litres/2 pts/5 cups vegetable stock

1 bay leaf

30 ml/2 tbsp chopped fresh coriander

30 ml/2 tbsp chopped fresh parsley

150 ml/¼ pt/⅔ cup milk

1 egg yolk

150 ml/¼ pt/⅔ cup single (light) cream

Salt and freshly ground black pepper

FOR THE CROÛTONS

4 slices of white bread, crusts removed

1 egg white, lightly beaten

25 g/1 oz stoned (pitted) black olives

25 g/1 oz stoned green olives

Sunflower or corn oil, for cooking

1 Melt the butter in a large saucepan. Add the spring onions and fry (sauté) for 2 minutes, stirring until softened but not browned.

2 Stir the vegetables and ground coriander into the pan and cook for 1 minute.

3 Add the stock and bay leaf. Bring to the boil, reduce the heat, part-cover and simmer gently for 20 minutes or until everything is tender.

4 Discard the bay leaf. Liquidise the soup in a blender or food processor with the fresh herbs and milk, then return to the pan.

5 Whisk the egg yolk with 120 ml/4 fl oz/½ cup of the cream. Whisk in two ladlefuls of the soup, then return this mixture to the pan and stir gently. Reheat but do not allow to boil or the mixture will curdle. Season to taste with salt and pepper.

6 While the soup is cooking, make the croûtons. Brush the slices of bread on both sides with the lightly beaten egg white.

7 Finely chop the olives in a blender or food processor, stopping and scraping down the sides as necessary. Sandwich the bread slices in pairs with the olives. Press firmly together. Cut into small cubes.

8 Heat oil for deep-frying to 190°C/375°F or until a piece of the discarded crust browns in 30 seconds. Fry the croûtons until golden, then drain on kitchen paper (paper towels).

9 Ladle the soup into warm bowls. Top each with a swirl of the remaining cream and a few croûtons and serve straight away.

Hints and variations If you don't like olives, fry plain cubes of bread in a mixture of oil and butter until golden, drain and serve on top of the soup.

Fresh figs
with Parma ham and Mozzarella

This Italian dish is an absolute café classic: luscious, sweet, ripe figs combined with creamy Mozzarella and best-quality prosciutto, garnished with fat black olives to give a sharp contrast of flavour and colour.

SERVES 6

6 fresh ripe figs, quartered

12 thin slices of Parma ham

6 baby balls of Mozzarella cheese, sliced

90 ml/6 tbsp olive oil

18 black olives

1 Arrange a quartered fig in a starburst pattern on each of six plates, with a gap in the centre.

2 Scrunch up the Parma ham gently and place in the centre.

3 Tuck the slices of Mozzarella between the pieces of fig.

4 Drizzle a little olive oil around each plate and put three black olives in the centre of the ham. Chill until ready to serve.

Serving suggestions Offer freshly ground black pepper and Melba toast with this dish.

Café style Mozzarella is a classic ingredient in Italian cooking. It is a pure white cheese and you should always buy the freshest you can find. The best is from around Naples, made into egg-shapes or plaited into ropes. It is made from water buffalos' milk and is always stored in its own whey to keep it moist and fresh. You can buy cows' milk Mozzarella, shaped and packed in the same way.

Avoid the blocks of Danish Mozzarella, which don't have the same moist, creamy texture.

Creamy mussels
with fennel and Pernod

Freshly caught mussels, steamed in white wine with finely chopped shallots and fennel, and served in their half-shells, in a pool of cooking juices laced with Pernod and enriched with crème fraîche. See photograph opposite page 24.

SERVES 6

1.75 kg/4 lb fresh mussels in their shells, scrubbed and beards removed

1 head of fennel

15 g/½ oz/1 tbsp butter

4 shallots, finely chopped

1 carrot, finely chopped

250 ml/8 fl oz/1 cup dry white wine

120 ml/4 fl oz/½ cup water

Salt and freshly ground black pepper

15 ml/1 tbsp cornflour (cornstarch)

30 ml/2 tbsp Pernod

120 ml/4 fl oz/½ cup crème fraîche

15 ml/1 tbsp chopped fresh parsley

1 Discard any cleaned mussels that are broken or open or don't close when sharply tapped.

2 Trim off the feathery fronds from the fennel, chop and reserve for garnish. Finely chop the fennel head. Heat the butter in a large saucepan. Add the shallots, fennel and carrot and fry (sauté), stirring, for 2 minutes until softened but not browned.

3 Stir in the wine and water and a good grinding of pepper. Add the mussels.

4 Bring to the boil, cover with a tight-fitting lid, reduce the heat to moderate and cook for 5–10 minutes or until the mussels open, shaking the pan occasionally. Discard any mussels that remain closed. Break off the top shells and discard.

5 Strain the cooking liquid into a clean pan.

6 Blend the cornflour with the Pernod and stir into the cooking liquid. Bring to the boil, stirring, then stir the crème fraîche. Taste and re-season, if necessary.

7 Pile the mussels into warm serving bowls. Pour the cooking liquid over the top. Sprinkle with the reserved chopped fennel fronds and parsley and serve.

Serving suggestions Offer your guests plenty of warm French bread to dip in the liquor, and soup spoons to drink the remainder.

Hints and variations This also makes a main meal for 3–4 people, served with a large bowl of chips (French fries) and a crisp green salad. If you prefer a more textured sauce, omit Step 5.

Crispy Castello on rocket
with fresh cranberry dressing

Wedges of creamy blue cheese, coated in egg and herbed crumbs, deep-fried and served on a bed of rocket with an olive oil, balsamic vinegar and fresh cranberry dressing.

SERVES 6

2 x 150 g/5 oz packs of Castello blue cheese, chilled

30 ml/2 tbsp cornflour (cornstarch)

1 egg, beaten

85 g/3½ oz/1 small packet of country-style stuffing mix

FOR THE DRESSING
60 ml/4 tbsp olive oil

15 ml/1 tbsp balsamic vinegar

60 ml/4 tbsp cranberry juice drink

Salt and freshly ground black pepper

75 g/3 oz fresh or thawed frozen cranberries

50 g/2 oz wild rocket, for garnishing

Sunflower or corn oil, for deep-frying

1 Cut each piece of cheese into three wedges. Dip in the cornflour, then the beaten egg, then the stuffing mix, to coat completely. Chill until ready to cook.

2 Whisk the olive oil with the vinegar and cranberry juice. Add a good pinch of salt and a generous grinding of black pepper. Stir in the cranberries and set aside until ready to serve.

3 Arrange the rocket on six plates.

4 Heat the oil for deep-frying to 190°C/375°F or until a cube of day-old bread browns in 30 seconds. Deep-fry the cheese for 1–2 minutes until golden brown and crisp. Drain on kitchen paper (paper towels).

5 Put a wedge of cheese on each plate, to one side of the rocket. Spoon the dressing over the leaves and serve straight away.

Serving suggestions A basket of soft white rolls will complete this course perfectly.

Hints and variations You can use Camembert instead of the blue Castello, if you prefer.

Photograph opposite:
Creamy Mussels with Fennel and Pernod (see page 23)

Tricolour melon cocktail
with Muscatel and ginger syrup and hot herb bread

Diced honeydew, cantaloupe and watermelon with chopped stem ginger, chilled and macerated in sweet Muscatel wine with the added kick of a dash of ginger syrup, served with hot, fragrant, herb bread.

SERVES 6

45 ml/3 tbsp syrup from a jar of stem ginger

250 ml/8 fl oz/1 cup Muscatel or other fruity sweet white wine

1 large wedge of watermelon

½ honeydew melon

1 small cantaloupe melon

4 pieces of stem ginger

FOR THE HERB BREAD
1 small French stick

75 g/3 oz/⅓ cup butter

15 ml/1 tbsp chopped fresh parsley

15 ml/1 tbsp chopped fresh basil

15 ml/1 tbsp snipped fresh chives

Small sprigs of fresh mint, for garnishing

1 Mix the ginger syrup and wine together in a large container.

2 Remove the seeds from all three melons. Either cut into dice or scoop into balls with a melon baller, discarding the rind.

3 Put the melon pieces in the syrup mixture. Chop the ginger and add. Mix well, cover and chill for at least 1 hour to macerate.

4 Meanwhile, make the bread. Cut the bread into 18 slices, not quite through to the base. Mash the butter with the herbs and spread between each slice. Wrap in foil and bake towards the top of a preheated oven at 220°C/425°F/gas 7/fan oven 200°C for about 10 minutes until the crust feels crisp when squeezed.

5 Spoon the melon and juices into six individual glass dishes. Garnish each with a small sprig of mint and serve with the hot herb bread.

Café style Set each glass dish on a large plate. Fold a small paper doily for each guest into a cone shape, tuck three slices of bread in each one and lay on the plates.

Photograph opposite:
Seared King Scallops with Spring Onions and Green Chillies (see page 38)

Bruschetta
with chicken livers, parsley and thyme

A delicious combination of Mediterranean flavours – chicken livers, lightly sautéed with dry vermouth and fresh parsley and thyme, piled on crisp slices of garlic-flavoured ciabatta.

SERVES 6

1 large garlic clove, halved

6 slices of ciabatta, cut diagonally from a large loaf

75 ml/5 tbsp olive oil

15 g/½ oz/1 tbsp butter

1 large onion, very finely chopped

450 g/1 lb chicken livers, trimmed and cut into bite-sized pieces

60 ml/4 tbsp dry white vermouth

45 ml/3 tbsp chopped fresh parsley

15 ml/1 tbsp chopped fresh thyme

Salt and freshly ground black pepper

1 Preheat the oven to 200°C/400°F/gas 6/fan oven 180°C.

2 Rub the cut garlic clove over both sides of each slice of bread, then discard the garlic. Brush the bread all over with some of the olive oil.

3 Place the bread on a baking (cookie) sheet and bake towards the top of the preheated oven for about 8 minutes until crisp and golden.

4 Meanwhile, heat 30 ml/2 tbsp of the oil with the butter in a large frying pan (skillet). Add the onion and fry (sauté), stirring, for 2 minutes until softened but not browned.

5 Add the chicken livers and fry, stirring, for about 3 minutes until just cooked but still pink and soft. Do not overcook or they will go hard.

6 Add the vermouth, half the parsley, the thyme and a little salt and pepper. Bubble rapidly until the vermouth has almost evaporated.

7 Place a slice of baked bread on each of six warm plates. Spoon the chicken liver mixture on top. Sprinkle with the parsley and serve immediately.

Café style For a special finishing touch, drizzle a little olive oil carefully round the edge of each plate.

Squid in prosciutto
with pesto vinaigrette

Tiny bundles of strips of tender baby squid and slivers of spring onions, wrapped in thin slices of pancetta, gently sautéed in olive oil and served with a fragrant pesto dressing spiked with lemon juice.

SERVES 6

12 cleaned baby squid tubes

1 bunch of spring onions (scallions)

12 thin slices of pancetta

FOR THE DRESSING
175 ml/6 fl oz/¾ cup olive oil

30 ml/2 tbsp pine nuts

45 ml/3 tbsp lemon juice

30 ml/2 tbsp chopped fresh basil

30 ml/2 tbsp freshly grated Parmesan cheese

45 ml/3 tbsp warm water

Salt and freshly ground black pepper

A little olive oil, for cooking

1 garlic clove, crushed

FOR THE GARNISH
Wedges of lemon

Sprigs of fresh basil

1 Check inside the cleaned squid tubes. If the tentacles and heads are there, remove them, then chop the tentacles and discard the heads. Slit the squid tubes and open out flat, then cut into thin strips lengthways. Rinse in cold water and pat dry with kitchen paper (paper towels).

2 Trim most of the green tops off the spring onions, then slice each onion lengthways into thin shreds.

3 Divide the squid and spring onions into 12 small bundles. Lay a slice of pancetta flat on the work surface, top with a bundle of squid and spring onion and wrap the pancetta firmly round the centre of each bundle.

4 Put 75 ml/5 tbsp of the oil in a blender or food processor with the pine nuts, 15 ml/1 tbsp of the lemon juice, the basil and cheese. Run the machine until smooth, stopping and scraping down the sides as necessary. Thin with the water. Season to taste with pepper.

5 Heat the remaining oil with the garlic in a large frying pan (skillet). Add the chopped tentacles, if using, then the squid bundles. Fry (sauté) gently for 4 minutes, then turn the bundles over and cook for a further 4 minutes until the pancetta is crisp and the squid is cooked.

6 Lift the squid bundles out of the pan and lay on warm plates. Stir the remaining lemon juice into the juices in the pan and season to taste. Spoon the juices over the squid. Drizzle the pesto dressing round the edge of each plate and garnish with a wedge of lemon and a small sprig of basil.

Serving suggestions Serve with pizza garlic bread or plain rolls.

Hints and variations For a simpler version, stuff the strips of spring onion into the squid tubes, leaving the ends poking out. Wrap the whole tube in the strip of pancetta, then continue as above.

Rainbow-peppered carpaccio
with wild rocket

Fillet steak rolled in freshly crushed multi-coloured peppercorns, sliced wafer-thin, drizzled with extra-virgin olive oil and fresh lemon juice, and garnished with shavings of fresh Parmesan and wild rocket.

SERVES 6

450 g/1 lb piece of thick fillet steak

15 ml/1 tbsp crushed rainbow peppercorns

50 g/2 oz wild rocket

120 ml/4 fl oz/½ cup extra-virgin olive oil

Thinly pared zest and juice of 1 lemon

50 g/2 oz/½ cup freshly shaved Parmesan cheese

1 Trim any sinews from the steak. Brush with 15 ml/1 tbsp of the olive oil, then roll in the peppercorns to coat thoroughly. Wrap in clingfilm (plastic wrap) and chill for 2 hours. Cut into thin slices.

2 Lay the slices two at a time between sheets of clingfilm and beat with a meat mallet or end of a rolling pin to flatten until wafer thin.

3 Arrange the slices, overlapping, round serving plates. Put a small pile of wild rocket in the centre.

4 Trickle the olive oil and lemon juice over and scatter with the Parmesan shavings. Scatter the lemon zest over the rocket and serve.

Serving suggestions Offer warm ciabatta bread and a large pat of fresh unsalted (sweet) butter.

Café style Peppercorns change colour as they mature, and the flavours also alter. 'Rainbow' peppercorns are a mixture of black, white, green and pink, green being the youngest and black fully mature. You may find them labelled 'Bristol blend', which also includes pimento for added flavour.

Crispy-wrapped tiger prawns
with sweet chilli and tomato salsa

Fresh tiger prawns wrapped in filo pastry and quickly deep-fried until crisp and golden, then garnished with fresh herbs, with a tangy sweet-and-spicy salsa to complete the feast of flavours.

SERVES 6

400 g/14 oz/1 large can of chopped tomatoes, drained

2 red chillies, seeded and finely chopped

60 ml/4 tbsp tomato ketchup (catsup)

20 ml/1½ tbsp balsamic vinegar

20 ml/1½ tbsp clear honey

Salt and freshly ground black pepper

9 sheets of filo pastry (paste)

36 raw peeled tiger prawns (jumbo shrimp), tails left on

Sunflower oil, for shallow-frying

Sprigs of fresh parsley, for garnishing

1 Mix the tomatoes, chillies, ketchup, vinegar and honey together. Season to taste with salt and pepper. Spoon into tiny individual dishes and chill until ready to serve.

2 Brush each piece of pastry with water. Fold in half, then cut, starting from the fold, into four equal strips.

3 Lay a prawn on each strip, with the tail projecting over the edge of the pastry. Wrap the pastry around the prawn to form a wedge-shaped parcel with a tiny tail end sticking out. Press the pastry firmly to seal the parcel.

4 Heat the oil in a large frying pan (skillet) and fry (sauté) the prawns in batches for about 1 minute on each side until golden brown and cooked. Drain on kitchen paper (paper towels) and keep warm while cooking the remainder.

5 Arrange the golden prawn parcels on large white plates, scatter with fresh green parsley, and set a tiny pot of the rich red salsa in the centre of each.

Mixed mushrooms with garlic
in a cream and Chardonnay sauce

A selection of the most flavoursome mushrooms, sautéed briefly in unsalted butter, then simmered in oak-aged Chardonnay, crushed garlic and fresh parsley, and finished with cream.

SERVES 6

700 g/1½ lb mixed mushrooms

4 shallots, finely chopped

50 g/2 oz/¼ cup unsalted (sweet) butter

300 ml/½ pt/1¼ cups oak-aged Chardonnay

Salt and freshly ground black pepper

2 large garlic cloves, finely chopped

45 ml/3 tbsp chopped fresh parsley

150 ml/¼ pt/⅔ cup double (heavy) cream

Sprigs of fresh flatleaf parsley, for garnishing

1 Trim the mushrooms, cutting up any that are very large, but leaving the majority whole. Rinse under cold running water and dry on kitchen paper (paper towels).

2 Fry (sauté) the shallots in the butter for 1 minute, stirring, until slightly softened.

3 Add the mushrooms and fry for 1 minute, stirring.

4 Add the Chardonnay and season lightly. Cover the pan with a lid or foil, reduce the heat and simmer gently for 10 minutes.

5 Sprinkle the garlic and parsley over the surface, re-cover and cook for a further 5 minutes.

6 Carefully remove the mushrooms with a draining spoon. Boil the cooking juices rapidly for 3 minutes until reduced by half. Add the cream to the pan juices, bring to the boil and cook rapidly, stirring all the time, until slightly thickened. Taste and re-season, if necessary. Return the mushrooms to the pan and heat through.

7 Spoon on to warm plates. Garnish each with a sprig of parsley and serve hot.

Serving suggestions Offer a basket of warm French bread to mop up the creamy juices.

Hints and variations Oyster, chestnut, chanterelle, morel, shiitake and button mushrooms are all suitable for this dish. Selection packs are available from supermarkets. Alternatively, you can use 12–18 large flat field or cultivated open mushrooms, peeled but left whole, for an equally delicious, if not quite so exotic, dish.

Golden croustades
with smoked salmon and caviar

Crisp, golden individual bread cases lined with smoked salmon and filled with fresh cream cheese and snipped fresh chives, lightened with crème fraîche, then topped with Avruga caviar.

SERVES 6

6 large slices of white bread, crusts removed

75 g/3 oz/⅓ cup butter, melted

200 g/7 oz/scant 1 cup cream cheese

60 ml/4 tbsp crème fraîche

30 ml/2 tbsp snipped fresh chives

Freshly ground black pepper

12 small square slices of smoked salmon

50 g/2 oz Avruga caviar

FOR THE GARNISH
A few twists of lemon

1 bunch of whole chive stalks

1 Preheat the oven to 190°C/375°F/gas 5/fan oven 170°C. Line six ramekin dishes (custard cups) with strips of non-stick baking parchment to help lift out the croustades after cooking.

2 Dip the bread in the melted butter to coat completely, then press into the ramekins.

3 Bake in the preheated oven at for about 30 minutes until crisp and golden brown. Using the parchment to help you, carefully remove the bread cases from the ramekins and set on a wire rack to cool.

4 Beat the cheese and crème fraîche together, then add the chives. Mix well and season with pepper. Chill.

5 When ready to serve, line each croustade with two slices of salmon, so the corners stick up out of the cases. Fill with the cheese mixture.

6 Spoon the caviar on top and serve garnished with twists of lemon and chive stalks.

Hints and variations Packs of ready-cut square slices of smoked salmon for sandwiches are available from supermarkets. For a delicious change, try filling the salmon-lined croustade with creamy scrambled egg instead of the cream cheese and chive mixture.

Café style Caviar certainly adds style to a dish, but who can afford the real thing? Avruga caviar makes an excellent, inexpensive alternative. It is actually herring roe, flavoured with a dash of lemon juice and a little salt. It has a delicious, slightly smoky flavour that many equate with Beluga caviar and it is far superior to the other well-known alternative to caviar, Danish lumpfish roe.

seafood main courses

Practically every country in Europe has its own special recipes for everything from wonderful shellfish to succulent whole fish cooked in a variety of imaginative ways to bring out the best of their flavours and textures.

Fish requires little cooking, so it is ideal for serving when you are entertaining guests. I have chosen many of these recipes for their added luxury factor, using fruits of the sea and freshwater fish that would not normally appear on your everyday menus. Each one is complemented with appropriate sauces and side dishes, and I've also suggested vegetable and salad accompaniments.

Mixed seafood pie
with a crisp filo topping

A fabulous selection of shellfish, squid and chunky cod fillet gently cooked in a rich tomato and white wine sauce, flavoured with leeks and garlic and topped with crisp, crumpled leaves of golden filo pastry.

SERVES 6

75 g/3 oz/⅓ cup butter

15 ml/1 tbsp olive oil

3 leeks, cut into small chunks

1 large onion, chopped

1 large garlic clove, crushed

700 g/1½ lb beefsteak tomatoes, skinned and chopped

5 ml/1 tsp caster (superfine) sugar

300 ml/½ pt/1¼ cups dry white wine

150 ml/¼ pt/⅔ cup fish stock

700 g/1½ lb mixed raw seafood, thawed if frozen

450 g/1 lb thick cod fillet, skinned and diced

Salt and freshly ground black pepper

150 ml/¼ pt/⅔ cup double (heavy) cream

6 large sheets of filo pastry (paste)

1 Melt the butter in a large saucepan, pour off half into a small pot and reserve. Add the oil to the remaining butter in the pan. Add the leeks, onion and garlic and cook gently, stirring, for 3 minutes until softened but not browned.

2 Add the tomatoes, sugar, wine and stock. Bring to the boil and cook for 5 minutes.

3 Add all the fish, stir gently, bring back to the boil, reduce the heat and cook gently for about 5 minutes until all the fish is cooked but still holding its shape. Season to taste and stir in the cream and 15 ml/1 tbsp of the parsley.

4 Meanwhile, brush a baking (cookie) sheet with a little of the reserved melted butter. Brush the sheets of filo with the rest of the butter, then scrunch each sheet gently to resemble crumpled paper. Place on the baking sheet. Bake in a preheated oven at 190°C/375°F/gas 5/fan oven 170°C for 5 minutes until golden and crisp.

5 Spoon the fish mixture on warm plates. Top each with a piece of the crumpled pastry.

Serving suggestion Serve with tiny buttered baby new potatoes and broccoli florets.

Café style For an attractive finishing touch, dust the edges of each plate with dried or finely chopped fresh parsley before placing the seafood and filo in the centre.

Grilled wild salmon and mangetout
with Muscadet and caviar sauce

Thick grilled salmon steaks, lightly seasoned with a mixture of lemon zest and celery salt, on a bed of steamed mangetout, surrounded by a sensational sauce made with Muscadet, cream and Avruga caviar.

SERVES 6

300 ml/½ pt/1¼ cups fish stock

300 ml/½ pt/1¼ cups Muscadet or other dry white wine

A good pinch of caster (superfine) sugar

120 ml/4 fl oz/½ cup double (heavy) cream

A pinch of ground white pepper

15 g/½ oz/2 tbsp Avruga caviar

350 g/12 oz mangetout (snow peas), topped and tailed

6 pieces of thick wild salmon fillet, about 175 g/6 oz each

15 g/½ oz/1 tbsp unsalted (sweet) butter, melted

5 ml/1 tsp celery salt

Finely grated zest of 1 small lemon

Freshly ground black pepper

1 First, make the sauce. Put the stock, Muscadet, sugar and cream in a saucepan. Bring to the boil and cook rapidly until reduced by half and thickened. Season the sauce with the pepper and stir in the caviar.

2 Put the mangetout in a steamer or metal colander over a pan of boiling water and steam for 3–5 minutes until just cooked but still with some 'bite', stirring once or twice.

3 Meanwhile, put the salmon fillets on foil on a grill (broiler) rack, skin-sides down. Brush with the butter and sprinkle with the celery salt and lemon zest. Grill (broil) for 6–8 minutes until cooked through and golden on top.

4 Arrange a small mound of mangetout in the centre of each warm plate. Top with a fillet of salmon and pour the sauce around.

Serving suggestion Serve with baby new potatoes, dressed with butter and finely chopped parsley. You could also offer a crisp green salad, if liked.

Café style Wild salmon has a much better flavour and texture and a more subtle colour than farmed salmon. However, you can use either in any recipe.

Poached sea bass in rosé wine
with saffron and prawn sauce

Fillets of sea bass, poached in Anjou rosé wine, which is then reduced to a delicious glossy jus flavoured with saffron, combined with crème fraîche and a generous helping of prawns and finally poured over the succulent fish.

SERVES 6

6 pieces of sea bass fillet, about 175 g/6 oz each

300 ml/¹/₂ pt/1¹/₄ cups Anjou rosé wine

300 ml/¹/₂ pt/1¹/₄ cups fish stock

1 bay leaf

6 black peppercorns

A good pinch of salt

5 ml/1 tsp saffron strands

150 ml/¹/₄ pt/²/₃ cup crème fraîche

175 g/6 oz cooked peeled prawns (shrimp)

5 ml/1 tsp lemon juice

FOR THE GARNISH
18 cooked unpeeled prawns

6 sprigs of fresh flatleaf parsley

1 Poach the fish in a shallow pan in the wine and stock with the bay leaf, peppercorns and salt for 6 minutes until just cooked through. Carefully lift the fish out of the pan and keep warm.

2 Add the saffron strands to the cooking liquid. Bring to the boil and cook rapidly for several minutes until reduced by half. Strain and return to the pan. Stir in the crème fraîche, cooked prawns and lemon juice. Taste and re-season.

3 Transfer the fish to warm plates and spoon a little of the sauce over. Garnish each plate with three cooked unpeeled prawns and a sprig of flatleaf parsley. Serve straight away.

Serving suggestion Buttered new potatoes make an ideal accompaniment, with a fresh green vegetable, such as sautéed courgettes (zucchini), or a crisp green salad to give added colour.

Café style You can buy saffron as strands or powder. The strands must be soaked in a little hot water or stock before use, as in this recipe, so for most dishes I prefer to use the powdered version, which avoids this, although it is not so easily available. Saffron is added to many rice and pasta dishes and sauces and may be used to flavour cakes and biscuits (cookies).

Monkfish and pancetta brochettes
with fresh tomato and avocado salsa

Moist chunks of meaty monkfish, flavoured with a tangy citrus marinade, wrapped in strips of pancetta, then grilled on skewers and served on a bed of colourful tomato and avocado salsa.

SERVES 6

1 lemon

1 lime

1 orange

90 ml/6 tbsp olive oil

15 ml/1 tbsp chilli oil

Salt and freshly ground black pepper

1 kg/2¼ lb monkfish tail, boned and cut into bite-sized chunks

24 thin slices of pancetta

FOR THE SALSA

3 beefsteak tomatoes

3 avocados

1 bunch of spring onions (scallions)

TO FINISH

50 g/2 oz/¼ cup butter

1 large garlic clove, crushed

30 ml/2 tbsp chopped fresh parsley

3 Mediterranean flat breads

6 sprigs of fresh flatleaf parsley

1 Finely grate the zest from the lemon and reserve. Squeeze the juice from all three citrus fruits. Mix half the juice with 75 ml/5 tbsp of the olive oil and the chilli oil in a shallow dish. Stir in the sugar and a little salt and pepper. Add the monkfish, turn to coat in the marinade and leave to marinate for 2 hours.

2 Cut the slices of pancetta in half.

3 Make the salsa. Cut the tomatoes into small dice and place in a bowl. Halve, peel and remove the stones (pits) from the avocados. Cut into small dice and add to the tomatoes. Trim the spring onions and chop finely. Add to the bowl and mix with the remaining juices, the lemon zest, the remaining olive oil and a pinch of salt. Chill until ready to serve.

4 Mash the butter with the garlic and parsley. Spread over each flat bread and lay them on a grill (broiler) rack, one at a time, if necessary. Grill (broil) until the butter melts. Wrap each in foil and keep warm until ready to serve.

5 Remove the fish from the marinade. Wrap each piece in a strip of pancetta, then thread on 12 soaked wooden skewers. Place on the grill rack and cook under a preheated grill for about 5 minutes, turning once and basting with the remaining marinade, until the pancetta is crisp and the fish cooked through.

6 Put a spoonful of salsa on to each of six large warm plates. Lay two skewers on top of the salsa. Cut the flat breads into wedges and arrange them on the side of each plate. Garnish the plates with sprigs of fresh flatleaf parsley and serve.

Serving suggestions This dish is quite sufficient on its own, but you could accompany it with new potatoes, wild rice or a crisp green salad, if you wish.

Crispy crab cakes
with tomato and chilli butter sauce

Crisp, golden cakes of crabmeat, fennel and rice, lightly sautéed and served with a buttery sauce flavoured with lime juice, fresh green chilli and chopped tomatoes.

SERVES 6

1 head of fennel

60 ml/4 tbsp water

175 g/6 oz/1½ cups cooked long-grain rice

350 g/12 oz white crabmeat

45 ml/3 tbsp mayonnaise

5 ml/1 tsp lemon juice

Salt and freshly ground black pepper

3 eggs, beaten

100 g/4 oz/2 cups fresh white breadcrumbs

1 lime

100 g/4 oz/½ cup unsalted (sweet) butter

1 fresh green chilli, seeded and finely chopped

2 tomatoes, skinned, seeded and finely chopped

15 ml/1 tbsp snipped fresh chives

25 g/1 oz/2 tbsp salted butter

60 ml/4 tbsp sunflower oil

1 Cut off the feathery fronds from the fennel and reserve for garnish. Finely chop the head and place in a small saucepan with the water. Cover and cook gently for 5 minutes to soften. If any water remains, boil rapidly, uncovered, until it has evaporated.

2 Mix the cooked rice with the crabmeat in a bowl. Add the fennel, mayonnaise, lemon juice and salt and pepper to taste. Mix gently but thoroughly. Add the beaten eggs to bind the mixture.

3 Shape the mixture into 18 small flat cakes. Coat in the breadcrumbs, then chill for at least 1 hour to firm.

4 Thinly pare the zest from the lime and squeeze the juice. Cut the zest into thin strips and boil in water for 2 minutes. Drain, rinse with cold water and drain again.

5 Melt the unsalted butter in a saucepan. Add the lime juice, chilli, tomatoes and chives and season lightly.

6 Heat the salted butter and sunflower oil in a large frying pan (skillet). Fry (sauté) the cakes in batches for 2–3 minutes on each side until crisp and golden. Drain each batch on kitchen paper (paper towels) and keep warm while cooking the remainder.

7 Reheat the lime and butter sauce. Arrange the fish cakes, in overlapping groups, clustered in the centres of large warm plates. Spoon the butter sauce around.

8 Garnish the plates with the reserved fennel fronds and the lime zest and serve straight away.

Serving suggestions I like these little cakes with lots of sauté potatoes and French (green) beans.

Hints and variations You can use fresh, frozen or canned crab meat for this recipe.

Seared king scallops
with spring onions and green chillies

Succulent, tender king scallops and their corals, seared in unsalted butter with finely chopped spring onions and green chillies, and served with wedges of lime to offset the richness. See photograph opposite page 25.

SERVES 6

100 g/4 oz/½ cup unsalted (sweet) butter

45 ml/3 tbsp olive oil

2 bunches of spring onions (scallions), finely chopped

2 large green chillies, seeded and finely chopped

36 king scallops with their corals

10 ml/2 tsp paprika

Salt and freshly ground black pepper

Finely grated zest and juice of ½ lime

FOR THE GARNISH
Whole chive stalks

Wedges of lime

1 Heat the butter and oil in a large frying pan (skillet). Fry (sauté) the spring onions and chillies for 3 minutes, stirring.

2 Add the scallops, sprinkle with the paprika, a little salt and pepper and the lime zest and juice and fry for 3 minutes, turning the scallops once.

3 Spoon the scallops and their juices on to large, flat plates. Garnish each one with a few chive stalks and wedges of lime and serve straight away.

Serving suggestions Steamed mangetout (snow peas) and a selection of salad leaves will complement this dish; or you could serve it with wild rice and a selection of plain seasonal baby vegetables.

Griddled tuna steaks
with a herb and anchovy vierge and baby chargrilled peppers

*Fresh tuna, lightly seasoned and seared on a griddle until just pink in the centre,
surrounded by a tangy anchovy, extra-virgin olive oil and fresh herb sauce, served
with smoky, chargrilled peppers.*

SERVES 6

50 g/2 oz/1 can of anchovies, drained

30 ml/2 tbsp milk

**120 ml/4 fl oz/½ cup extra-virgin
olive oil**

15 ml/1 tbsp lemon juice

**15 ml/1 tbsp fresh chopped
coriander (cilantro)**

15 ml/1 tbsp fresh chopped parsley

18 baby (bell) peppers of any colour

6 tuna steaks, about 150 g/5 oz each

2.5 ml/½ tsp salt

5 ml/1 tsp paprika

Freshly ground black pepper

Coarse sea salt

FOR THE GARNISH
Thin sprigs of fresh flatleaf parsley

1 To make the vierge, soak the anchovies in the milk for 15 minutes to
remove the saltiness. Drain, then mash the anchovies well with a
fork in a small saucepan. Using a balloon whisk, work in 90 ml/
6 tbsp of the oil, then add the lemon juice and chopped herbs. Heat
gently until the anchovies melt into the oil. Remove from the heat.

2 Put the peppers under a preheated grill (broiler) and cook, turning
occasionally, for about 10 minutes until the skin is blackened. Place
them all in a plastic bag to cool. When cool enough to handle, peel
off the skins. Wrap in foil and keep warm.

3 Mix the salt and paprika with a good grinding of pepper. Brush the
tuna with oil on both sides, then sprinkle with the paprika mix.

4 Heat a large griddle pan until very hot, then cook the tuna for
2–3 minutes on each side until cooked but still pink in the centre.

5 Quickly reheat the vierge. Transfer the tuna to warm plates and
spoon the vierge over. Arrange the peppers attractively at one side
and sprinkle with coarse sea salt. Garnish the plates with sprigs of
fresh parsley and serve.

Serving suggestions A green salad will provide further contrasts of
colour and texture and buttered noodles or baby new potatoes will
complete the dish.

Plaice and oysters in crispy sesame batter
with caper and tarragon mayonnaise

Tender strips of plaice wrapped around fresh oysters, fried in a light batter flavoured with the oyster juices and toasted sesame seeds, and served with a herby, piquant mayonnaise.

SERVES 6

18 fresh oysters in their shells

6 small plaice fillets, skinned

FOR THE MAYONNAISE
300 ml/¹/₂ pt/1¹/₄ cups mayonnaise

10 ml/2 tsp sesame oil

Finely grated zest and juice of ¹/₂ lemon

30 ml/2 tbsp chopped fresh tarragon

30 ml/2 tbsp chopped capers

Freshly ground black pepper

FOR THE SESAME BATTER
90 ml/6 tbsp sesame seeds

175 g/6 oz/1¹/₂ cups plain (all-purpose) flour

100 g/4 oz/1 cup cornflour (cornstarch)

30 ml/2 tbsp baking powder

2.5 ml/¹/₂ tsp salt

A little cold water

Corn oil, for deep-frying

FOR THE GARNISH
Nasturtium flowers

Wedges of lemon

1 Shuck the oysters (see below) and drain the liquid into a jug. Take the oysters out of their shells and pat dry on kitchen paper (paper towels). Warm the deep shells in a very low oven.

2 Cut each plaice fillet into three strips. Roll one around each oyster and secure with a wooden cocktail stick (toothpick).

3 Mix the mayonnaise ingredients thoroughly together and season to taste. Spoon into six small serving dishes.

4 Dry-fry the sesame seeds in a frying pan (skillet), stirring until lightly toasted. Tip out of the pan into a mixing bowl.

5 Sift the flours with the baking powder and salt into the bowl. Make the oyster liquid up to 300 ml/½ pt/1¼ cups with cold water. Stir into the flour mixture to form a fairly thin but still creamy batter.

6 Heat the oil for deep-frying to 190°C/375°F or until a cube of day-old bread browns in 30 seconds. Dip the plaice rolls in the batter to coat thinly, then deep-fry for about 3 minutes until crisp and golden. Drain on kitchen paper and carefully remove the cocktail sticks.

7 Transfer the fish rolls to the oyster shells and arrange three with a bowl of mayonnaise on each of six plates. Garnish the plates with nasturtium flowers and wedges of lemon and serve straight away.

Serving suggestions This is so elegant, it needs only the plainest accompaniments, such as sauté potatoes and a mixed salad.

Hints and variations To shuck an oyster, hold it firmly in one hand, protected by a thick cloth or oven glove. Insert a sharp knife between the two shells and push against the hinge, twisting until it breaks. Open the oyster carefully to avoid spilling the juices and loosen it from the shell with the knife.

Sautéed trout fillets
with soft-boiled quails' eggs and fine asparagus

Delicate fillets of trout, pan-fried in butter with flaked almonds, served on a bed of tender asparagus spears and lightly cooked quails' eggs, with a sophisticated light Dijon mustard dressing.

SERVES 6

12 quails' eggs

225 g/8 oz fine baby asparagus spears

FOR THE DRESSING
10 ml/2 tsp Dijon mustard

15 ml/1 tbsp cider vinegar

45 ml/3 tbsp olive oil

A good pinch each of salt, freshly ground black pepper and caster (superfine) sugar

FOR THE FISH
50 g/2 oz/¼ cup unsalted (sweet) butter

50 g/2 oz/½ cup flaked (slivered) almonds

6 large trout fillets, halved lengthways

Juice of ½ lemon

Salt and freshly ground black pepper

30 ml/2 tbsp chopped fresh parsley

1 Put the quails' eggs in a pan of cold water. Bring to the boil, cook for 30 seconds only, then quickly remove and plunge in a bowl of cold water to prevent further cooking.

2 Put the asparagus in an even layer in a steamer or metal colander that will fit over a saucepan. Steam the asparagus for 5 minutes or until just tender. Shell the quails' eggs and cut each one in half.

3 Make the dressing. Put all the ingredients in a bowl and whisk until thick and well blended.

4 Melt the butter in two large frying pans (skillets), add the trout, skin-side up, and fry (sauté) for 2 minutes. Carefully turn over and fry for a further 2 minutes until cooked through. Scatter the almonds in the pan and allow to brown briefly while the trout finishes cooking.

5 Arrange the asparagus and quails' eggs on warm plates. Top each with two pieces of trout fillet. Add the lemon juice, a little salt and pepper and the parsley to the trout juices, bring to the boil and spoon over the fish.

6 Trickle the dressing round the edges of the plates and serve.

Serving suggestions Baby new potatoes, cooked in their skins, make a simple, tasty side dish that is quick to prepare.

Gratin of baked crab
with a golden cheese topping

Whole crabs, served in their shells, dressed with brandy and crème fraîche and seasoned with a dash of Tabasco, with a golden baked breadcrumb and Cheddar cheese topping.

SERVES 6

6 cooked dressed crabs

50 g/2 oz/¼ cup unsalted (sweet) butter, melted

Finely grated zest of 1 small lemon

10 ml/2 tsp Dijon mustard

15 ml/1 tbsp brandy

90 ml/6 tbsp crème fraîche

A few drops of Tabasco sauce

Freshly ground black pepper

50 g/2 oz/1 cup fresh white breadcrumbs

75 g/3 oz/¾ cup finely grated Cheddar cheese

FOR THE GARNISH
Wedges of lemon

Small sprigs of fresh parsley

1 Preheat the oven to 220°C/425°F/gas 7/fan oven 200°C.

2 Scoop all the crabmeat out of the shells into a large bowl. Add half the melted butter, the lemon zest, mustard, brandy, crème fraîche, a few drops of Tabasco and a good grinding of pepper. Mix together gently, taking care not to break up the chunks of white crabmeat too much. Spoon the mixture back into the crab shells.

3 Mix the remaining melted butter with the breadcrumbs and cheese. Spoon over the tops of the crabs and press down very gently.

4 Transfer to a large baking (cookie) sheet. Bake in the preheated oven for 10 minutes until golden and piping hot.

5 Garnish each crab with a small sprig of parsley and put a wedge of lemon on the plate. Serve.

Serving suggestions Keep the accompaniments simple: plain new potatoes and a crisp green salad are perfect.

Hints and variations If you buy cooked crabs that have not been dressed, remove the bodies from the shells, discarding the dead men's fingers. Scoop all the meat from the shells, pick out all the meat from the bodies and crack the large claws and remove the meat. Break off the inner piece of the underside of the shell at the natural line and continue as above.

Café style You can make these look spectacular by serving them in large white paper napkins. Lay each napkin out flat, then fold in half to form a large triangle. Fold the point of the triangle down to the long edge opposite. Take the two side points and draw them together, tying them in a half-knot. Place one napkin on each large plate with the knot in front and lay a crab inside so that it looks as though the napkin is wrapped gently round it.

Hake with pan-roasted onions and pimenton
on crushed potatoes with garlic

*Succulent hake steaks topped with pimenton-flavoured roasted Spanish onions,
served on a bed of roughly crushed potatoes, flavoured with garlic and enriched with
double cream.*

SERVES 6

1 kg/2¼ lb potatoes, peeled and cut
into chunks

350 g/12 oz extra-fine French
(green) beans

2 garlic cloves, crushed

30 ml/2 tbsp double (heavy) cream

6 thick hake steaks,
about 175 g/6 oz each

2 large bay leaves

Salt and freshly ground black pepper

3 large Spanish onions,
halved and sliced

90 ml/6 tbsp olive oil

25 g/1 oz/2 tbsp butter

7.5 ml/1½ tsp sweet pimenton

1 Boil the potatoes in lightly salted water for about 15 minutes or until tender. Steam the beans in a steamer or colander over the potatoes for about 10 minutes until tender, stirring once. Drain the potatoes thoroughly and return to the saucepan. Leave the beans covered, ready to reheat before serving.

2 Add the garlic and cream to the potatoes. Crush roughly with a fork until broken up but not finely mashed. Cover the pan and keep warm until ready to serve.

3 Meanwhile, put the fish in a large frying pan (skillet). Add the bay leaves, a little salt and pepper and just enough water to cover. Bring to the boil, reduce the heat and cook gently for 6 minutes until tender.

4 In a separate pan, fry (sauté) the onions in the oil and the butter for 6 minutes, stirring, until soft and golden. Add the pimenton and some pepper.

5 Pour boiling water over the beans to reheat.

6 Spoon the crushed potato mixture on to six warm plates. Top each with a hake steak and spoon the onions and their juices on top. Arrange the beans in a criss-cross pattern to one side and serve.

Serving suggestions A fresh, cool tomato salad will add a delicious contrast of colour and texture.

Café style Pimenton is not very commonly used, but it is available in good supermarkets. It gives this dish a lovely rich, smoky, slightly sweet, peppery flavour. It is a Spanish red paprika made from a blend of peppers that have been smoked, dried and ground. There are three types, sweet, bitter-sweet and hot. There is also a less smoky version made in the French Basque country. You can substitute Hungarian paprika, but the flavour won't be so distinctive.

Lobster Newburg
with buttered mixed rice

Succulent, freshly cooked lobster in an amontillado sherry sauce enriched with egg yolks and single cream, served on a colourful bed of buttery white and Camargue red rice.

SERVES 6

3 small cooked lobsters

2 lemons

350 g/12 oz/1½ cups long-grain rice

100 g/4 oz/½ cup Camargue red rice

75 g/3 oz/⅓ cup unsalted (sweet) butter

175 ml/6 fl oz/¾ cup amontillado sherry

4 egg yolks

300 ml/½ pt/1¼ cups single (light) cream

1.5 ml/¼ tsp cayenne

Salt and freshly ground black pepper

60 ml/4 tbsp chopped fresh parsley

Paprika, for dusting

1 Twist the legs and claws off the lobsters. Reserve the legs for garnishing. Crack the claws and remove the meat. Using a large, sharp knife, split each lobster in half down the back, then remove the gills from behind the head and the black vein that runs down the length of the body. Remove all the meat from the body and cut into neat pieces.

2 Thinly pare the zest from the lemons, cut into thin strips and boil in water for 2 minutes, drain, rinse with cold water and drain again. Squeeze the juice.

3 Cook the two varieties of rice together in plenty of boiling, lightly salted water for 10 minutes until tender but still with a little 'bite'. Drain, rinse with boiling water and drain again, then add 25 g/1 oz/ 2 tbsp of the butter and toss gently.

4 Melt the remaining butter in a saucepan. Add the lobster and toss gently for about 3 minutes until hot through but not brown. Add the sherry and lemon juice and boil rapidly until reduced by half.

5 Beat the egg yolks with the cream, cayenne and a little salt and pepper and add to the pan. Cook over a gentle heat until thickened but do not allow to boil.

6 Spoon the buttered rice on to warm serving plates. Spoon the lobster mixture on top. Sprinkle the lemon zest over the lobster. Dust the edges of the plates with paprika and chopped parsley and arrange the claws attractively to one side. Serve hot.

Serving suggestions I would serve this with a crisp green salad, to offset the richness of the sauce.

meat and poultry main courses

Café-style main courses vary enormously from light and fanciful to robust and filling. That's because some are based on rustic, regional food that kept the agricultural workers well fed, while others include the little delicacies that graced the tables of the landowners and gentry. If you're choosing one of the more substantial dishes make sure you choose a light starter so your guests can do it justice!

All these recipes include everything you need – such as sauces and accompaniments – to serve a complete main course. I've also suggested extra vegetables or salads that will complement the whole dish. Most of the work can be done in advance and, once cooked, many of these dishes will sit happily for some time, covered loosely with foil, in a low oven.

Lamb shank in redcurrant jus

with celeriac mash

Whole shanks of this season's lamb, slow-cooked with garlic and rosemary until meltingly tender, then bathed in a rich wine and redcurrant jus on a bed of celeriac and potato mash.

SERVES 6

6 lamb shanks

2 garlic cloves, cut into thin slivers

30 ml/2 tbsp fresh chopped rosemary

Salt and freshly ground black pepper

300 ml/¹/₂ pt/1¹/₄ cups meat stock

300 ml/¹/₂ pt/1¹/₄ cups red wine

1 kg/2¹/₄ lb potatoes, cut into chunks

1 large celeriac (celery root), cut into chunks

25 g/1 oz/2 tbsp butter

45 ml/3 tbsp redcurrant jelly (clear conserve)

15 ml/1 tbsp tomato purée (paste)

30 ml/2 tbsp brandy

FOR THE GARNISH
6 sprigs of fresh rosemary

6 small sprigs of fresh redcurrants

1 Preheat the oven to 160°C/325°F/gas 3/fan oven 145°C.

2 Make small slits in the lamb shanks with the point of a sharp knife and insert the slivers of garlic.

3 Place in a large roasting tin (pan). Sprinkle with the rosemary and some salt and pepper. Pour the stock and wine around.

4 Cover the tin tightly with foil and bake in the preheated oven for 3 hours until very tender.

5 When the meat is almost cooked, cook the potatoes and celeriac together in boiling, lightly salted water for about 10–15 minutes until tender. Drain thoroughly, then mash with the butter and a good grinding of black pepper.

6 Carefully lift the lamb shanks out of the tin and keep warm. Spoon off any excess fat from the cooking juices. Stir in the redcurrant jelly and tomato purée until dissolved, then add the brandy. Bring to the boil and cook for 1 minute, stirring. Taste and re-season, if necessary.

7 Pile up the celeriac mash in the centre of six large, warm plates. Rest a lamb shank against each pile of mash. Spoon the redcurrant jus over.

8 Stand a sprig of rosemary up in each pile of mash right next to the lamb and cluster a sprig of redcurrants on the lamb next to the rosemary. Serve straight away.

Serving suggestions Plain steamed green vegetables go best with a rich dish such as this – try mangetout (snow peas) or petit pois.

Roast rack of lamb and baby leeks
with a Madeira and mint demi-glace

Racks of sweet, tender lamb cutlets roasted on a bed of baby leeks and served with a reduction of the pan juices, enhanced with Madeira, balsamic vinegar and chopped fresh mint.

SERVES 6

6 racks of lamb, each with 4 cutlets

Salt and freshly ground black pepper

10 ml/2 tsp dried mint

18 baby leeks, trimmed

30 ml/2 tbsp olive oil

300 ml/½ pt/1¼ cups meat stock

90 ml/6 tbsp Madeira

10 ml/2 tsp clear honey

45 ml/3 tbsp chopped fresh mint

15 ml/1 tbsp balsamic vinegar

Sprigs of fresh mint, for garnishing

1 Preheat the oven to 220°C/425°F/gas 7/fan oven 200°C.

2 Score the skin of each rack of lamb in a criss-cross pattern. Rub with a little salt and pepper, then sprinkle with the dried mint.

3 Blanch the trimmed leeks in boiling, lightly salted water for 2 minutes. Drain thoroughly. Place in a large roasting tin (pan) and drizzle with the oil. Place the racks of lamb on top.

4 Roast towards the top of the preheated oven for 20 minutes.

5 Transfer the leeks and lamb to warm plates and keep warm.

6 Add the stock, Madeira, fresh mint and vinegar to the pan juices and boil rapidly, stirring, for 3 minutes until reduced and syrupy. Season to taste. Spoon over the lamb, garnish with sprigs of fresh mint and serve.

Serving suggestions To complete this elegant roast meal, I would serve baby roast potatoes and cauliflower cheese.

Honey-glazed gammon steaks
with white wine and dill sauce and black pepper mash

Lean, tender honey-glazed gammon steaks, set on piles of fluffy potatoes seasoned with coarsely ground black peppercorns, surrounded by a creamy mustard sauce, flavoured with dill and white wine.

SERVES 6

1 kg/2¼ lb potatoes, cut into small chunks

65 g/2½ oz/scant ⅓ cup butter

15 ml/1 tbsp single (light) cream

10 ml/2 tsp black peppercorns, crushed or coarsely ground

Salt

6 lean gammon steaks

45 ml/3 tbsp sunflower oil

30 ml/2 tbsp clear honey

300 ml/½ pt/1¼ cups medium-dry white wine

30 ml/2 tbsp chopped fresh dill (dill weed)

45 ml/3 tbsp Dijon mustard

250 ml/8 fl oz/1 cup crème fraîche

A pinch of caster (superfine) sugar

Sprigs of fresh dill, for garnishing

1 Cook the potatoes in lightly salted, boiling water until tender. Drain and return to the pan. Mash thoroughly with a potato masher, then beat in half the butter, the cream and crushed or coarsely ground black pepper. Season to taste with salt.

2 Meanwhile, snip the edges of the gammon all round to prevent curling during cooking. Brush the steaks with the oil on one side. Heat a griddle pan until very hot, then sear each steak for 3 minutes on one side only. Remove from the pan.

3 Brush the uncooked sides with oil and the honey. Reheat the griddle pan and cook the honey-glazed sides for 3 minutes or until cooked through and glazed. Remove from the pan and keep warm, glazed sides up.

4 To make the sauce, put the wine in a saucepan and boil rapidly for about 4 minutes until reduced by half. Stir in the dill, mustard and crème fraîche. Bring to the boil and boil for 2 minutes until thickened. Season to taste with salt, pepper and the sugar.

5 Put a pile of mash on each of six warm plates. Make a tiny well in the centre and put in a small knob of butter so it melts into a pool. Set a gammon steak beside the mash, just slightly propped up. Spoon a little sauce on to the steak (don't smother it), allowing the sauce to trickle on to the plate. Garnish each plate with a sprig of dill.

Serving suggestions I like to serve this with plain baby vegetables, such as broad (fava) beans and carrots.

Photograph opposite:
Pork Escalopes with Cider and Mustard Sauce on Savoy and Apple Rosti (see page 52)

Pistachio and herb-crusted pork chops
with orange-butter-glazed persimmons

Lean and tender pork loin chops, coated in a crisp sage and pistachio nut crumb crust and served with grilled slices of sweet and sharp persimmon, bathed in orange-flavoured butter.

SERVES 6

100 g/4 oz/1 cup shelled pistachio nuts, skinned (see page 130)

100 g/4 oz/2 cups fresh white breadcrumbs

30 ml/2 tbsp chopped fresh sage

30 ml/2 tbsp chopped fresh parsley

10 ml/2 tsp dried onion granules

Salt and freshly ground black pepper

6 large lean boneless pork loin chops

2 large eggs, beaten

3 ripe orange persimmons

Finely grated zest and juice of 1 orange

50 g/2 oz/¼ cup butter, melted

75 ml/5 tbsp sunflower oil

A few sprigs of fresh parsley, for garnishing

1 Reserve half the nuts for garnishing and chop the remainder.

2 Mix the breadcrumbs with the herbs, chopped nuts, onion granules and some salt and pepper.

3 Dip the chops in the beaten egg, then the crumb mixture, to coat completely.

4 Heat the oil in two frying pans (skillets). Add the chops and cook over a moderate heat for about 4 minutes on each side until crisp, golden and cooked through. Drain on kitchen paper (paper towels).

5 Meanwhile, cut the tops off the persimmons and cut into slices. Mix the orange zest and juice with the melted butter. Lay a piece of foil on a grill (broiler) rack and brush with some of the butter. Lay the persimmons on the foil and brush with more of the butter. Cook under a preheated grill for 4–5 minutes, turning once and brushing with more butter, until lightly golden round the edges.

6 Transfer the cooked pork to warm plates. To one side, lay the persimmon slices, just overlapping, and drizzle any remaining orange butter over. Garnish with a few reserved pistachio nuts and sprigs of fresh parsley and serve.

Serving suggestions I like to serve these with plenty of sautéed potatoes and French (green) beans.

Hints and variations The crumb mixture can be made very simply in a food processor. Just drop the pieces of bread in first, then add the nuts, then the herbs and seasonings.

Photograph opposite:
Sautéed Duck Breasts with Red Onion and Kumquat Marmalade (see page 59)

Smoked pork and venison sausage cassoulet
with a garlic and herb crust

A robust yet surprisingly refined blend of colourful mixed pulses, smoked pork loin and venison sausages, slow-braised in a white wine stock with button mushrooms and whole baby onions, and topped with a golden crumb crust.

SERVES 6

350 g/12 oz dried bean mix, soaked in
cold water overnight

15 ml/1 tbsp olive oil

12 button (pearl) onions, peeled
but left whole

6 venison sausages, cut into chunks

350 g/12 oz smoked pork loin,
cut into chunks

1 garlic clove, crushed

225 g/8 oz baby button mushrooms

600 ml/1 pt/2½ cups meat stock

300 ml/½ pt/1¼ cups dry white wine

1 bouquet garni sachet

Salt and freshly ground black pepper

FOR THE CRUMB CRUST
40 g/1½ oz/3 tbsp butter

100 g/4 oz/2 cups fresh
white breadcrumbs

45 ml/3 tbsp chopped fresh parsley

45 ml/3 tbsp chopped fresh thyme

1 garlic clove, crushed

1 Preheat the oven to 160°C/325°F/gas 3/fan oven 145°C.

2 Drain the beans and place in a saucepan. Cover with cold water. Bring to the boil and cook rapidly for 10 minutes. Drain.

3 Heat the oil in a large flameproof casserole (Dutch oven). Add the button onions and chunks of sausage and brown quickly on all sides. Add the beans with the pork loin, garlic, mushrooms, stock, wine, bouquet garni and some salt and pepper.

4 Cover tightly with a lid and cook in the oven for 3½ hours until the beans and meat are cooked and richly bathed in sauce. Discard the bouquet garni. Taste and re-season.

5 Spoon the mixture into six individual ovenproof serving dishes.

6 Melt the butter and mix with the breadcrumbs, herbs, garlic and a little salt and pepper. Spoon the crumb mixture over the top of each dish and press down lightly.

7 Place the little casseroles in the oven. Turn up the heat to 190°C/375°F/gas 5/fan oven 170°C and bake for 35 minutes until crisp and golden on top.

Serving suggestions A crisp green salad makes a simple but perfect accompaniment.

Hints and variations You can use other speciality sausages instead of the venison ones and for more variety, use equal quantities of smoked bacon and fresh pork instead of the smoked pork loin.

Café style Wrap a white linen napkin round each pot before serving.

Pork tonnata
with flageolet beans

*Marinated pork escalopes, cooked in olive oil, oregano and celery, then chilled,
smothered in a piquant tuna and anchovy mayonnaise and served with creamy pale
green flageolet beans.*

SERVES 6

175 g/6 oz/1 cup dried flageolet beans,
soaked in cold water for several hours

Salt and freshly ground black pepper

1 shallot, very finely chopped

30 ml/2 tbsp finely chopped fresh parsley

Finely grated zest and juice of
1 large lemon

6 slices of pork fillet,
about 150 g/5 oz each

45 ml/3 tbsp olive oil

1 large bay leaf

7.5 ml/1½ tsp dried oregano

1 celery stick, chopped

A good pinch of celery salt

FOR THE TONNATA
2 x 85 g/3½ oz/small cans of tuna,
drained

2 x 50 g/2 oz/small cans of anchovy
fillets, drained

4 egg yolks

175 ml/6 fl oz/¾ cup extra-virgin olive
oil, plus extra for drizzling

30 ml/2 tbsp capers

6 sprigs of fresh flatleaf parsley,
for garnishing

1 Drain the soaked beans. Place in a pan and cover with cold water. Bring to the boil and boil rapidly for 10 minutes. Reduce the heat, part-cover and simmer gently for about 45 minutes or until tender. Add a good pinch of salt, leave to stand for 5 minutes, then drain, rinse with cold water and drain again.

2 Mix with the shallot, parsley and 5 ml/1 tsp of the lemon zest. Season with salt and pepper. Chill.

3 Put the slices of pork fillet, one at a time, into a plastic bag and beat with a rolling pin or meat mallet until flattened. Place in a large, shallow dish. Add the oil, bay leaf, oregano, celery, celery salt, the remaining lemon zest and a good grinding of pepper. Turn gently to coat, then leave to marinate for 2 hours.

4 Meanwhile, put the tuna in a blender or food processor with the anchovies and the lemon juice. Blend until smooth. Add the egg yolks and blend again. With the machine running, add the measured olive oil a trickle at a time, until thick and glossy. Season to taste. Turn into a covered container and chill.

5 Heat a large griddle. Lift the escalopes out of the marinade. Cook them quickly for about 3 minutes on each side until seared and cooked through. Transfer to a platter and allow to cool, then chill.

6 When ready to serve, pile a spoonful of the beans to the side of each of six plates. Drizzle with olive oil. Lay a pork escalope, slightly propped up, on the beans. Spoon a little mayonnaise mixture over the pork, not obscuring it completely, with the rest spilling across the plates. Scatter the capers over. Garnish with sprigs of fresh flatleaf parsley and serve.

Serving suggestions Complete the meal with some warm crusty bread and a rocket salad.

Pork escalopes with cider and mustard sauce
on savoy and apple rosti

Thin slivers of pork tenderloin, flash-fried in butter, served in a piquant sauce of dry cider, cream and grainy mustard with a golden cake of shredded Savoy cabbage, King Edward potatoes and sweet apple. See photograph opposite page 48.

SERVES 6

½ small Savoy cabbage, finely shredded

450 g/1 lb potatoes

3 red eating (dessert) apples

1 green eating apple

1 small onion

Salt and freshly ground black pepper

90 ml/6 tbsp sunflower oil

10 ml/2 tsp lemon juice

550 g/1¼ lb pork tenderloin

5 ml/1 tsp dried sage

25 g/1 oz/2 tbsp unsalted (sweet) butter

450 ml/¾ pt/2 cups dry vintage cider

15 ml/1 tbsp grainy mustard

150 ml/¼ pt/⅔ cup double (heavy) cream

6 small sprigs of fresh parsley or sage, for garnishing

1 Blanch the cabbage in boiling water for 3 minutes. Drain and pat dry on kitchen paper (paper towels).

2 Peel and coarsely grate the potatoes, squeeze well to remove the excess liquid, then add to the cabbage. Coarsely grate two of the red apples, including the skin, and add to the potatoes and cabbage. Grate the onion and add to the bowl. Mix together thoroughly and season well.

3 Shape the mixture into six flat cakes. Heat the oil in two frying pans (skillets), add the potato cakes and fry (sauté) for 10 minutes until crisp and golden underneath. Turn over and cook for a further 10 minutes until golden and cooked through. Transfer to a warm dish.

4 Halve, core and thinly slice the remaining apples. Toss the slices in lemon juice to prevent browning and reserve for garnishing.

5 Cut the pork tenderloin into fine slices – you need 30 pieces in all, so halve them if necessary. Place the slices a few at a time in a plastic bag and beat with a rolling pin or meat mallet until flattened and thin. Season them with a little salt and pepper and the sage.

6 Heat the butter in a frying pan. Fry the pork in batches quickly on both sides until browned and cooked through. Transfer to a plate and keep warm.

7 Pour the cider into the pork cooking juices. Bring to the boil and boil rapidly until reduced by half. Stir in the mustard and cream and season to taste. Bring to the boil.

8 Transfer the potato cakes to warm plates. Arrange overlapping slices of pork to one side. Spoon some of the grainy mustard jus over the pork, arrange a few slices of apple attractively to one side with a sprig of parsley or sage and serve straight away.

Serving suggestions Serve with broccoli and baby carrots.

Fillet steaks in pâté butter filo parcels
with tawny port sauce

*Tender fillet steaks baked in delicate leaves of filo pastry, layered with smooth liver
pâté-flavoured butter, and served with a rich port jus flavoured with Mediterranean
mixed herbs.*

SERVES 6

6 fillet steaks, about 150 g/5 oz each

Salt and freshly ground black pepper

75 g/3 oz/⅓ cup butter

15 ml/1 tbsp olive oil

75 g/3 oz smooth liver pâté

6 large sheets of filo pastry (paste)

30 ml/2 tbsp cornflour (cornstarch)

300 ml/½ pt/1¼ cups beef stock

75 ml/5 tbsp tawny port

15 ml/1 tbsp balsamic vinegar

2.5 ml/½ tsp Mediterranean dried mixed herbs

Sprigs of fresh watercress, for garnishing

1 Preheat the oven to 190°C/375°F/gas 5/fan oven 170°C.

2 Season the steaks lightly with salt and pepper. Melt 15 g/1 tbsp of the butter in a large frying pan (skillet). Add the olive oil and heat. When very hot, sear the steaks quickly on both sides. If you like your steaks well done, turn down the heat and cook for a further 5 minutes, turning once.

3 Mash 25 g/1 oz/2 tbsp of the remaining butter with the pâté and beat well until fairly soft. Melt the last of the butter.

4 Lay a sheet of filo on a board. Dot half the sheet with a sixth of the pâté butter and fold the other half of the pastry over the top. Put a steak in the middle and gather up the edges of the pastry to form a pouch. Transfer the pouch to a baking (cookie) sheet and brush with a little of the melted butter. Repeat to make six pouches, brushing each with melted butter. Bake the pouches in the preheated oven for 15 minutes until crisp and golden.

5 Meanwhile, stir the cornflour into the juices in the frying pan. Gradually blend in the stock, port and balsamic vinegar and add the herbs. Bring to the boil and cook for 1 minute, stirring. Season to taste.

6 Spoon a pool of the port jus on to each of six warm plates. Top each with a steak parcel. Garnish the plates with sprigs of fresh watercress and serve straight away.

Serving suggestions Try these with sauté potatoes and a green vegetable, such as broccoli.

Hints and variations You can make the parcels in advance, then chill until ready to bake. For a change, make these 'country-style' by mashing the butter with crumbled Stilton cheese instead of the pâté.

Braised beef in Chianti
with baby onions, carrots and pancetta

Thick slices of lean, tender steak, gently braised with button onions, carrots and cubes of Italian pancetta in a smooth and rich sauce flavoured with red wine, herbs and brandy.

SERVES 6

6 thick slices of lean braising steak, about 225 g/8 oz each

25 g/1 oz/¼ cup plain (all-purpose) flour

Salt and freshly ground black pepper

120 ml/4 fl oz/½ cup olive oil

18 button onions, peeled but left whole

2 garlic cloves, crushed

3 carrots, sliced

100 g/4 oz diced pancetta

300 ml/½ pt/1¼ cups beef stock

½ bottle of Chianti

5 ml/1 tsp caster (superfine) sugar

15 ml/1 tbsp sun-dried tomato purée (paste)

45 ml/3 tbsp brandy

1 bouquet garni sachet

6 slices of bread, crusts removed

45 ml/3 tbsp chopped fresh parsley, for garnishing

1 Preheat the oven to 180°C/350°F/gas 4/fan oven 160°C.

2 Trim any fat or sinews from the meat. Season the flour with a little salt and pepper and toss the meat in the mixture to coat.

3 Heat half the oil in a large flameproof casserole (Dutch oven) and brown the onions on all sides. Remove with a draining spoon.

4 Add the pieces of braising steak, two at a time, and brown quickly on both sides. Add the garlic, carrots and pancetta to the pan and cook for 1 minute, stirring. Stir in any remaining flour and blend in the stock, wine, sugar, tomato purée and brandy. Bring to the boil, stirring.

5 Return the meat and onions to the sauce. Tuck in the bouquet garni.

6 Cover and transfer to the preheated oven and cook for 2 hours or until meltingly tender.

7 Discard the bouquet garni, taste and re-season, if necessary.

8 Meanwhile, cut the bread into triangles. Fry (sauté) in the remaining oil until crisp and golden on both sides. Drain on kitchen paper (paper towels).

9 Carefully lift the meat slices on to six warm plates. Spoon the sauce and vegetables over. Arrange four triangles of fried bread around the edge of each and sprinkle the meat with chopped parsley.

Serving suggestions This country-style dish is best given very simple accompaniments – either some warm ciabatta bread and a green salad or perhaps jacket-baked potatoes, with crème fraîche and chive dressing, if you like, and broccoli.

Slivered fillet steak with onions
in a brandy, crème fraîche and green peppercorn sauce

Tender morsels of fillet steak, sautéed with plenty of thinly sliced onions, then flambéed with brandy and finally simmered in crème fraîche with piquant green peppercorns.

SERVES 6

450 g/1 lb/2 cups long-grain rice

150 g/5 oz/²⁄₃ cup butter

4 large onions, halved and thinly sliced

1 kg/2¼ lb fillet steak, cut into thin strips

75 ml/5 tbsp brandy

450 ml/³⁄₄ pts/2 cups crème fraîche

30 ml/2 tbsp pickled green peppercorns

Salt

45 ml/3 tbsp chopped fresh parsley

FOR THE GARNISH
6 sprigs of fresh parsley

2 small onions, thinly sliced and separated into rings

1 Cook the rice in plenty of boiling, salted water for 10 minutes or until just tender, then drain, rinse with boiling water and drain again. Toss in 50 g/2 oz/¼ cup of the butter and keep warm.

2 Melt half the remaining butter in a very large frying pan (skillet). Add the onions and fry (sauté), stirring, for 4 minutes until soft and only slightly golden. Remove from the pan.

3 Melt the remaining butter in the pan. Add the steak strips and fry quickly for 3–4 minutes, stirring, until cooked through and browned.

4 Return the onions to the pan and stir in gently. Add the brandy and ignite. Shake the pan until the flames subside. Add the crème fraîche and peppercorns and cook gently for 2 minutes. Season to taste.

5 Put a bed of rice on each of six warm plates. Spoon the beef mixture in the centre. Sprinkle with chopped parsley. Put a sprig of parsley and a few onion rings to one side to garnish.

Serving suggestions A plain green vegetable, such as some fine green beans, or a green salad will set off the rich sauce of this dish perfectly.

Seared sirloin steaks
with salsa verde

Tender sirloin steaks, simply seasoned and grilled to your liking, served with a fresh, slightly peppery sauce made with watercress, herbs and olive oil, spiked with chopped cornichons.

SERVES 6

1 bunch of watercress

50 g/2 oz fresh parsley

40 g/1½ oz/¾ cup fresh white breadcrumbs

150 ml/¼ pt/⅔ cup olive oil, plus extra for brushing

4 cornichons

60 ml/4 tbsp lemon juice

30 ml/2 tbsp snipped fresh chives

6 sirloin steaks

Salt and freshly ground black pepper

200 ml/7 fl oz/scant 1 cup beef stock

A few chive stalks, for garnishing

1 To make the salsa, trim and discard the feathery ends from the watercress stalks, then place the sprigs in a blender or food processor with the parsley, breadcrumbs, olive oil, cornichons, lemon juice and snipped chives. Run the machine until finely chopped and well blended, stopping and scraping down the sides as necessary. Season to taste.

2 Brush the steaks with olive oil and season on both sides. Heat a griddle pan until hot. Add the steaks and cook for 2–5 minutes on each side, depending on how well you like your steaks cooked. Transfer to warm plates.

3 Add the stock to the pan and quickly scrape up any sediment between the ridges of the griddle. Bring it back to the boil, taste and season, if necessary. Trickle these pan juices over the steaks.

4 Spoon the salsa around and garnish each plate with a few chive stalks. Serve straight away.

Serving suggestions Everyone loves steak and chips – so I would always serve French fries with this (you can cheat and use very thin oven chips), plus some petit pois and baby carrots.

Hints and variations When cooking steaks or duck that require only the briefest searing, cook one side in advance, then just finish cooking the other side at the last minute before serving.

Parma chicken
with mushroom and Romano pepper compôte

Corn-fed chicken breasts stuffed with creamy Bel Paese cheese, tomatoes and fresh basil, wrapped in Parma ham and baked, then served with a compôte of mushrooms and sweet red Romano peppers.

SERVES 6

6 corn-fed chicken breasts, skinned

175 g/6 oz Bel Paese cheese

3 plum tomatoes, sliced

12 fresh basil leaves

Salt and freshly ground black pepper

6 thin slices of Parma ham

90 ml/6 tbsp olive oil

FOR THE COMPÔTE

450 g/1 lb button mushrooms, sliced

2 Romano peppers, sliced

2 garlic cloves, crushed

150 ml/¼ pt/⅔ cup tomato juice

150 ml/¼ pt/⅔ cup red wine

15 ml/1 tbsp Worcestershire sauce

2.5 ml/½ tsp caster (superfine) sugar

2.5 ml/½ tsp dried oregano

30 ml/2 tbsp chopped fresh parsley

Sprigs of fresh basil, for garnishing

1 Preheat the oven to 190°C/375°F/gas 5/fan oven 170°C.

2 Wipe the chicken breasts and make a slit along the side of each with a sharp knife, to form a deep pocket.

3 Fill with the cheese and tomatoes and push in two basil leaves into each one. Season with pepper and wrap in a piece of Parma ham.

4 Lay the chicken breasts in a baking tin (pan) and brush all over with 45 ml/3 tbsp of the olive oil. Add 45 ml/3 tbsp of water to the tin. Bake in the preheated oven for 30 minutes until the chicken is cooked through.

5 Meanwhile, heat the remaining oil in a large saucepan. Add the mushrooms and peppers and cook, stirring, for 3 minutes. Add all the remaining compôte ingredients except the parsley. Bring to the boil and cook fairly rapidly for 8–10 minutes, stirring occasionally, until thickened and glazed. Stir in the parsley and season to taste.

6 Transfer the chicken breasts to warm plates. Cut each one into five slices and fan out slightly. Spoon any pan juices over. Spoon the compôte to one side and garnish each plate with a sprig of basil. Serve straight away.

Serving suggestions Arrange a pile of buttered noodles or couscous on each plate beside the chicken breast slices and accompany with a crisp green salad.

Hints and variations If you prefer a moister dish, dress the cooked noodles with plenty of passata (sieved tomatoes) flavoured with 2.5 ml/½ tsp of dried basil and some salt and pepper.

Café style Romano peppers are a great favourite of mine. They are longer and more pointed than ordinary (bell) peppers, and they have a particularly good, sweet flavour.

French-roasted spring chicken
with golden potatoes, mushrooms and wilted spinach

*Spatchcocked poussins, roasted in butter and olive oil with whole baby new potatoes
and cup mushrooms, subtly flavoured with young, fresh garlic, flatleaf parsley and
toasted pine nuts, served with the buttery pan juices on a bed of wilted spinach.*

SERVES 6

6 poussins (Cornish hens)

50 g/2 oz/¼ cup unsalted (sweet) butter

**450 g/1 lb baby Charlotte potatoes,
scrubbed**

225 g/8 oz cup mushrooms, sliced

Salt and freshly ground black pepper

3 fresh garlic cloves, finely chopped

**45 ml/3 tbsp chopped fresh
flatleaf parsley**

45 ml/3 tbsp toasted pine nuts

450 ml/¾ pt/2 cups chicken stock

450 g/1 lb baby spinach

1 Preheat the oven to 180°C/350°F/gas 4/fan oven 160°C.

2 Using poultry shears or a sharp knife, cut down both sides of the
backbone of each poussin and discard the bone. Gently open each
bird out flat.

3 Heat half the butter in a large frying pan (skillet). Brown the birds,
two at a time.

4 Place all the poussins in a large roasting tin (pan). Heat the
remaining butter in the frying pan and brown the potatoes on all
sides, then add the mushrooms and stir. Tip into the pan with the
poussins and season with salt and pepper. Cover the tin with foil
and cook in the preheated oven for 45 minutes.

5 Sprinkle the garlic, parsley and pine nuts over the chicken, re-cover,
then cook for a further 5 minutes.

6 Transfer the poussins, potatoes and mushrooms to a warm platter
and keep warm.

7 Add the chicken stock to the pan. Bring to the boil and cook rapidly
until reduced by half. Season to taste.

8 Meanwhile, wash the spinach well. Add to a pan of boiling water,
bring back to the boil, then remove from the heat and drain
thoroughly in a sieve (strainer). Press to remove all the excess water.

9 Spoon a bed of spinach on to each of six warm plates. Arrange the
poussins on top of the spinach with the potatoes and mushrooms
around and spoon the pan juices over. Garnish each plate with a
sprig of flatleaf parsley and serve.

Serving suggestions This dish has everything you need, but you
could offer some warm French bread and a tomato salad if you wish.

Sautéed duck breasts
with red onion and kumquat marmalade

Young Barbary duck breasts, seared in a pan, served with sweet red onions and sliced tart kumquats, simmered in red wine vinegar and demerara sugar until soft and stickily glazed. See photograph opposite page 49.

SERVES 6

50 g/2 oz/¼ cup butter

3 red onions, thinly sliced

9 kumquats

15 ml/1 tbsp demerara sugar

60 ml/4 tbsp caster (superfine) sugar

120 ml/4 fl oz/½ cup pure orange juice

30 ml/2 tbsp red wine vinegar

6 small Barbary duck breasts, with skin

Salt and freshly ground black pepper

15 ml/1 tbsp cornflour (cornstarch)

300 ml/½ pt/1¼ cups chicken stock

15 ml/1 tbsp mushroom ketchup (catsup)

5 ml/1 tsp chopped fresh sage

6 small sprigs of fresh parsley, for garnishing

1 Melt half the butter in a saucepan. Add the onions and fry (sauté), stirring, for 3 minutes. Very thinly slice three of the kumquats and add to the pan with the sugar. Continue to cook, stirring occasionally, for about 5 minutes until the onions and kumquats are soft and deep golden brown.

2 Stir in half the orange juice and the vinegar. Stir for 1 minute until rich and thick. Remove from the heat.

3 Using a sharp knife, remove the sinew that runs from the pointed end of the underside of the duck breasts. This stops them curling up when cooked. Season the duck with salt and pepper.

4 Heat the remaining butter in a large frying pan (skillet), add the duck breasts, skin-sides down, and fry for about 5 minutes until golden brown. Turn over and cook for a further 3 minutes. They will be just pink in the middle. If you prefer your duck well done, cook for another 2 minutes. Remove from the pan and keep warm.

5 Spoon off all but 15 ml/1 tbsp of fat from the pan. Stir in the cornflour. Blend in the remaining orange juice, the stock, mushroom ketchup and sage. Bring to the boil and cook for 1 minute, stirring. Season to taste.

6 Meanwhile, reheat the onion marmalade and halve the remaining kumquats.

7 Cut each breast diagonally into six slices and arrange on warm plates. Spoon the pan juices over. Add a spoonful of the marmalade to one side and garnish each plate with two halves of kumquat and a small sprig of parsley.

Serving suggestions With the tang of the marmalade, this dish needs only the gentlest of flavours to complement it. Try baby new potatoes, braised celery or green beans and petit pois.

Pan-braised pheasant
with puy lentils and chestnuts

Pheasant portions, braised with chestnuts, carrots and onions, glazed with a reduced jus flavoured with oloroso sherry and served on a bed of small green lentils.

SERVES 6

3 carrots

45 ml/3 tbsp olive oil

3 oven-ready pheasants, halved

2 onions, finely chopped

1.2 litres/2 pts/5 cups chicken stock

200 g/7 oz cooked peeled chestnuts, quartered

1 bay leaf

Salt and freshly ground black pepper

175 g/6 oz/1 cup puy lentils

45 ml/3 tbsp sweet sherry

25 g/1 oz/2 tbsp unsalted (sweet) butter

30 ml/2 tbsp chopped fresh parsley

Sprigs of fresh parsley, for garnishing

1 Preheat the oven to 180°C/350°F/gas 4/fan oven 160°C.

2 Shave one carrot into long ribbons using a potato peeler. Blanch the ribbons in boiling water for 1 minute to soften slightly, then roll up to form rosettes. Reserve for garnish. Finely dice the remaining carrots.

3 Heat the oil in a large flameproof casserole (Dutch oven), add the pheasant halves and brown, then remove. Put the onions and carrots into the casserole and cook for 2 minutes, stirring.

4 Add 600 ml/1 pt/2½ cups of the stock, the chestnuts, bay leaf and a little salt and pepper. Return the pheasant halves to the pan. Bring to the boil, reduce the heat and cover.

5 Braise in the preheated oven for 1 hour until tender.

6 Meanwhile, cook the lentils in the remaining stock for about 25 minutes or until tender, adding a little water, if necessary, to prevent drying.

7 When the pheasant halves are cooked, carefully lift out of the pan and keep warm. Discard the bay leaf. Take out the chestnuts, carrots and onions with a draining spoon and add to the lentils. Taste and season, if necessary.

8 Add the sherry to the juices in the pan and boil rapidly until reduced by half, then whisk in the butter, a little piece at a time. Taste and re-season, if necessary.

9 Put the lentil mixture on six warm plates. Top each with a pheasant half. Spoon the sherry juices over and garnish each plate with a few carrot rosettes and a sprig of parsley.

Serving suggestions I like to serve this with a colourful selection of fresh baby vegetables in season.

pizzas, pasta and rice

No café menu would be complete without a small selection of tasty and authentic pizzas, some fresh pastas and beautifully presented rice dishes. These are predominantly influenced by Italian cookery methods, of course, but touches from the rest of the Mediterranean still keep appearing! Apart from the rice cakes, where I have given a serving suggestion, all these dishes need is a crisp, dressed green salad and, for those who need more to fill them up, some garlic bread (made with either Italian flat breads or a French stick).

Pizza fiorentina

A thin and crispy pizza, topped with tomatoes, fresh spinach, grated nutmeg, garlic, oregano, grated Mozzarella and a free-range egg, and scattered with Parmesan shavings.

PIZZAS, PASTA AND RICE

SERVES 6

FOR THE PIZZA DOUGH
450 g/1 lb plain (all-purpose) flour

5 ml/1 tsp salt

5 ml/1 tsp caster (superfine) sugar

15 g/½ oz/1 sachet of easy-blend dried yeast

30 ml/2 tbsp olive oil, plus extra for greasing

300 ml/½ pt/1¼ cups hand-hot water

FOR THE TOPPING
120 ml/4 fl oz/½ cup passata (sieved tomatoes)

500 g/18 oz fresh spinach

2.5 ml/½ tsp grated nutmeg

1 large garlic clove, finely chopped

5 ml/1 tsp dried oregano

225 g/8 oz/2 cups grated Mozzarella cheese

6 eggs

30 ml/2 tbsp extra-virgin olive oil

50 g/2 oz/½ cup freshly shaved Parmesan cheese

1 Mix the flour, salt, sugar and yeast in a bowl. Add the olive oil and mix with the water to form a firm dough. Knead on a lightly floured surface for 5 minutes until smooth and elastic. Alternatively, put all the ingredients except the water in a food processor. Run the machine, gradually adding the water until the dough is formed, then continue to run the machine for 1 minute.

2 Put the dough in an oiled plastic bag and leave in a warm place for 1 hour to rise. Meanwhile, preheat the oven to 220°C/425°F/gas 7/fan oven 200°C.

3 Knock back (punch down) the dough and divide into six equal pieces. Roll out each piece to an oval about 23 cm/9 in long. Place each oval on a double thickness of foil, leaving a 'handle' of foil sticking out at each end to make lifting easier. Spread each with passata, not quite to the edges.

4 Bake, three to a shelf, towards the top of the oven for 10 minutes.

5 Meanwhile, wash the spinach thoroughly. Cook in a saucepan with just the water clinging to its leaves for 5 minutes. Drain and squeeze out as much moisture as possible. Snip with scissors, then spread out on the six part-cooked pizzas. Sprinkle with the nutmeg, garlic and oregano, then scatter the Mozzarella over.

6 Make a slight well in the centre of each topping and break an egg into it. Drizzle with the olive oil. Return to the oven to cook for 10 minutes until the pizzas are golden round the edges, the cheese has melted and is browning slightly and the eggs are set. Scatter the Parmesan over and serve straight away.

Hints and variations I have made the pizzas in ovals rather than rounds to accommodate six in the oven.

Café style For the best flavour, go for fresh Mozzarella, made from buffalos' milk.

Pizza marinara

A traditional-style, thin-based pizza topped with passata, fresh tomatoes, garlic, olive oil, oregano, Mascarpone cheese and fresh basil, piled with fresh wild rocket just before serving.

SERVES 6

1 quantity of pizza dough (see page 62)

120 ml/4 fl oz/½ cup passata (sieved tomatoes)

6 tomatoes, thinly sliced

2 garlic cloves, finely chopped

350 g/12 oz/1½ cups Mascarpone cheese

5 ml/1 tsp dried oregano

6 sprigs of fresh basil, torn into small pieces

Freshly ground black pepper

90 ml/6 tbsp olive oil

100 g/4 oz wild rocket

1 Make up the dough (see page 62) and leave to rise for 1 hour. Knock back (punch down) and divide into six equal pieces.

2 Preheat the oven to 220°C/425°F/gas 7/fan oven 200°C.

3 Roll out each piece of dough to an oval, about 23 cm/9 in long. Place each base on a double thickness of oiled foil, with enough foil sticking out at each end to aid lifting.

4 Spread with the passata, then top with the tomatoes and garlic. Put three small mounds of cheese on each pizza and spread out. Sprinkle with the oregano, basil and some pepper. Drizzle with the olive oil.

5 Bake the pizzas, three to a shelf, towards the top of the preheated oven for 20 minutes until risen and golden round the edges.

6 Slide on to warm plates. Pile the fresh rocket on top and serve straight away.

Hints and variations You can make round pizzas if you prefer, although the oval ones are easier to fit into the oven if you are cooking for six.

Calzone

A thin pizza dough, smothered in garlic butter, anchovies, grated courgettes, olives, fresh sage and three cheeses, folded in half and baked until the filling is piping hot, with all the flavours and aroma ready to burst out when the crust is broken.

SERVES 6

1 quantity of pizza dough (see page 62)

100 g/4 oz/½ cup unsalted (sweet) butter, softened

2 large garlic cloves, crushed

2 large courgettes (zucchini), coarsely grated

2 x 50 g/2 oz/small cans of anchovies, drained

100 g/4 oz sliced stoned (pitted) black olives

45 ml/3 tbsp chopped fresh sage

75 g/3 oz/¾ cup grated Cheddar cheese

75 g/3 oz/¾ cup grated Mozzarella cheese

175 g/6 oz/¾ cup ricotta cheese

Freshly ground black pepper

30 ml/2 tbsp olive oil, plus extra for greasing

1 egg, beaten

25 g/1 oz/2 tbsp freshly grated Parmesan cheese

1 Make up the dough (see page 62) and leave to rise. Knock back (punch down) and divide into six equal pieces. Roll out each piece to a 20 cm/8 in round.

2 Preheat the oven to 220°C/425°F/gas 7/fan oven 200°C.

3 Mash the butter with the garlic and spread over half of each piece of dough, not quite to the edges. Squeeze the grated courgettes to remove any excess moisture, then spread over. Top with the anchovies, olives, sage and cheeses. Season each one well with black pepper and drizzle with olive oil.

4 Brush the edges with beaten egg, fold over and press to seal. Transfer to two oiled baking (cookie) sheets. Brush with beaten egg.

5 Bake in the preheated oven for about 20 minutes until crisp and golden, swapping the positions of the baking sheets halfway through cooking. Serve hot, dusted with grated Parmesan cheese.

Hints and variations I like the glazed look that the beaten egg gives but it's not strictly authentic so, if you prefer, brush with water to seal the edges together and brush the top with olive oil before baking. This is also delicious filled with cooked spinach and ricotta cheese. Spread the calzone with 350 g/12 oz of ricotta. Prepare the spinach as for Pizza Fiorentina (see page 62), then spread over the ricotta. Add 2 chopped onions sautéed in olive oil with a crushed garlic clove. Fold and cook as above.

Café style Soft ricotta cheese has a lovely mild flavour. *Ricotta* is an Italian word that literally means 're-cooked'. Whey left after making hard cheese is reheated, then fresh milk is added to make a cheese that is suitable for sweet and savoury dishes.

Cosa nostra

Pizza dough parcels, filled with ham, green beans, pimientos, pepperoni,
mushrooms, Mozzarella cheese, capers and oregano, baked until puffy and golden
and served with a smooth tomato sauce and freshly grated Parmesan.

SERVES 6

1 quantity of pizza dough (see page 62)

FOR THE FILLING
75 g/3 oz cooked ham, finely diced

75 g/3 oz pepperoni sausage,
thinly sliced

75 g/3 oz cooked French (green) beans,
cut into short lengths

425 g/15 oz/1 large can of pimiento
caps, drained well and chopped

75 g/3 oz button mushrooms, sliced

225 g/8 oz Mozzarella cheese, sliced

30 ml/2 tbsp capers

10 ml/2 tsp dried oregano

Salt and freshly ground black pepper

30 ml/2 tbsp olive oil,
for brushing and greasing

FOR THE SAUCE
600 ml/1 pt/2½ cups passata
(sieved tomatoes)

5 ml/1 tsp dried basil

2.5 ml/½ tsp caster (superfine) sugar

50 g/2 oz/½ cup freshly grated
Parmesan cheese

Sprigs of fresh basil, for garnishing

1 Make up the dough (see page 62), leave to rise, then knock back (punch down). Divide into six equal pieces and roll out each to a round about 20 cm/8 in in diameter.

2 Preheat the oven to 200°C/400°F/gas 6/fan oven 180°C.

3 Pile all the filling ingredients in the centre of each round of dough.

4 Brush the edges with water and draw them up over the filling, pinching them well together to form a parcel.

5 Place the parcels seam-sides down on a lightly oiled baking (cookie) sheet. Brush all over with olive oil.

6 Bake in the preheated oven for about 25 minutes until golden and cooked through.

7 Meanwhile, put the passata, garlic, basil, sugar and a little salt and pepper in a saucepan. Heat through.

8 Transfer the parcels to warm plates. Spoon a little sauce over the centres, then around the plates. Sprinkle with Parmesan, garnish with sprigs of fresh basil and serve.

Café style There are two types of Parmesan: Reggiano and Grand Padano. Parmigiano Reggiano is the higher-prized of the two and is made only in a small, restricted part of Italy. It has a flaky texture and a delicious, nutty flavour that goes well with bread and red wine. Gran Padano is made in other regions and is grainier in texture, as well as stronger and saltier.

Linguine with baby plum tomatoes
in a chilli cream brandy and Amaretto sauce

Baby plum tomatoes simmered in olive oil, butter and chillies, finished with cream, brandy and a splash of Amaretto and served on a bed of thin ribbon pasta and garnished with crisp Parmesan wafers. See photograph opposite page 72

SERVES 6

100 g/4 oz/1 cup freshly grated Parmesan cheese

75 g/3 oz/⅓ cup unsalted (sweet) butter

60 ml/4 tbsp olive oil, plus extra for greasing

2 small red chillies, seeded and chopped

450 g/1 lb baby plum tomatoes, halved

45 ml/3 tbsp tomato purée (paste)

120 ml/4 fl oz/½ cup water

120 ml/4 fl oz/¼ cup double (heavy) cream

45 ml/3 tbsp brandy

30 ml/2 tbsp Amaretto liqueur

Salt and freshly ground black pepper

700 g/1½ lb fresh linguine

A small handful of torn flatleaf parsley or a few basil leaves, for garnishing

1 Preheat the oven to 200°C/400°F/gas 6/fan oven 180°C and oil a baking (cookie) sheet.

2 Put spoonfuls of grated Parmesan cheese on the sheet in 12 small piles, spaced well apart so that they have room to spread. Flatten each one slightly. Bake in the preheated oven for 10 minutes until melted. Remove from the oven and leave to cool and become crisp.

3 Heat the butter and oil in a saucepan. Add the chillies and tomatoes and cook for 1 minute only.

4 Blend the tomato purée with the water and add to the tomatoes with the cream, brandy and Amaretto and bring to the boil. Remove from the heat and season to taste.

5 Cook the linguine according to the packet directions. Drain and return to the pan.

6 Bring the sauce back to the boil, add to the pasta and toss gently.

7 Spoon into warm pasta bowls. Garnish with torn flatleaf parsley or basil leaves and put two Parmesan wafers, slightly overlapping, in the side of each bowl.

Hints and variations Don't serve extra Parmesan with this dish as it will mask the subtle flavours.

Café style Parmesan is the most important hard cheese in Italian cuisine. For the best flavour, always use it fresh, from a block. It can be grated or shaved, and because it does not become stringy when cooked, it is excellent for sauces, stuffings, toppings, coatings and garnishes.

Mafaldine
with smoked salmon and broccoli

Wide ribbon pasta, cooked and folded through sautéed shallots, tiny broccoli florets and strips of oak-smoked salmon, and finished with crème fraîche, eggs and a dash of anchovy essence.

SERVES 6

550 g/1¼ lb mafaldine

350 g/12 oz broccoli, broken into tiny florets

6 shallots, finely chopped

25 g/1 oz/2 tbsp unsalted (sweet) butter

350 g/12 oz smoked salmon pieces, cut into narrow strips

4 eggs

150 ml/¼ pt/⅔ cup milk

300 ml/½ pt/1½ cups crème fraîche

15 ml/1 tbsp anchovy essence (extract)

Salt and freshly ground black pepper

A squeeze of lemon juice

45 ml/3 tbsp chopped fresh parsley

50 g/2 oz/½ cup freshly shaved Parmesan cheese

1 Cook the mafaldine in plenty of boiling, lightly salted water according to the packet directions until just al dente. Add the broccoli for the last 4 minutes' cooking time. Drain thoroughly.

2 In the same large pan, fry (sauté) the shallots very gently in the butter for 3 minutes, stirring until softened but not browned. Tip the pasta and broccoli back into the pan, add the smoked salmon and stir gently.

3 Beat the eggs with the milk, crème fraîche and anchovy essence. Add to the pan and turn and stir gently over a low heat until bathed in sauce and hot through. Don't overcook – the eggs should still be creamy, not scrambled. Add seasoning and lemon juice to taste and then add the parsley.

4 Pile the pasta into warm bowls, add the Parmesan shavings and serve.

Café style Don't throw the rind away when you've finished a block of fresh Parmesan. It can be used to add flavour to stock or soup. You can substitute Pecorino, another hard Italian cheese, which is slightly cheaper, in any recipe calling for Parmesan.

Giant asparagus and ricotta ravioli
with creamy tomato and bacon sauce

Pillows of freshly made egg pasta, generously filled with fresh asparagus, ricotta cheese, fresh parsley and basil, served in a tomato and bacon sauce, flavoured with oregano and enriched with cream.

SERVES 6

FOR THE PASTA
4 large eggs

400 g/14 oz/3½ cups strong (bread) flour

60 ml/4 tbsp water

Flour, for dusting

FOR THE FILLING
450 g/1 lb fresh asparagus

450 g/1 lb/2 cups ricotta cheese

30 ml/2 tbsp chopped fresh basil

30 ml/2 tbsp chopped fresh parsley

Finely grated zest of ½ lemon

Salt and freshly ground black pepper

1 Put the eggs in a food processor and run the machine for about 30 seconds. Add the flour and water and run the machine until the mixture forms a soft but not sticky dough.

2 Knead gently on a lightly floured surface until smooth and elastic. Place in an oiled plastic bag and leave to rest for 30 minutes while you make the filling.

3 Trim the bases of the asparagus stalks, and scrape if thick. Cut in half, if long. Either boil in salted water or steam until just tender (the time will depend on the thickness of the stalks). Tip into a sieve (strainer), rinse with cold water and drain well.

4 Reserve 12 spear ends of asparagus for garnishing. Pat the remainder dry on kitchen paper (paper towels), then tip into a food processor and run the machine until the asparagus is finely chopped but not puréed. (You can do this by hand if you prefer.) Work in the cheese, herbs, lemon zest and salt and pepper to taste.

5 Cut the dough in half. Roll out each half very thinly to a rectangle about 45 x 30 cm/18 x 12 in. Cut in half.

6 Spoon half the asparagus mixture at regular intervals to make 12 piles in even rows over one piece of dough. Brush around each pile with water and place a second dough rectangle on top. Press gently between each mound and around the edges to seal. Use a pastry wheel or sharp knife to cut into 12 large ravioli. Carefully put to one side and leave to dry while you repeat the process with the remaining filling and two pieces of dough.

FOR THE SAUCE

1 large onion, finely chopped

100 g/4 oz rashers (slices) of streaky bacon, rinded and finely chopped or minced (ground)

30 ml/2 tbsp olive oil

600 ml/1 pt/2½ cups passata (sieved tomatoes)

2.5 ml/½ tsp dried oregano

150 ml/¼ pt/⅔ cup double (heavy) cream

50 g/2 oz/½ cup freshly grated Parmesan cheese

7 Make the sauce. Fry (sauté) the onion and bacon gently in the oil for about 4 minutes until the onion is soft and the bacon is cooked but not browned. Add the passata, oregano and cream and season to taste with salt and pepper. Bring to the boil and simmer for 3 minutes.

8 Bring a large pan of salted water to the boil. Drop in eight of the ravioli, one at a time, and boil for 4–5 minutes, until the pasta is cooked and has risen to the surface. Carefully lift out with a draining spoon. Drain well and place on a warm plate. Cover with foil and keep warm while cooking the remainder. When all the ravioli are cooked, transfer to warm pasta bowls. Spoon the sauce over, dust with grated Parmesan, lay two reserved asparagus spears on top of each and serve.

Hints and variations I use a food processor to chop the onion and bacon for the sauce. Make sure you discard any sinewy stringy bits of bacon that don't chop properly.

Lasagne
with beef and Mediterranean vegetables

*Layers of rich beef and red wine ragoût, chopped red and green peppers,
aubergines, courgettes and tomatoes and sheets of lasagne, topped with a delicate
béchamel sauce and dusted with freshly grated Parmesan cheese.*

SERVES 6

FOR THE RAGOÛT
1 large onion, chopped

2 garlic cloves, crushed

75 ml/5 tbsp olive oil

500 g/18 oz extra-lean minced
(ground) steak

300 ml/½ pt/1¼ cups beef stock

150 ml/¼ pt/⅔ cup red wine

30 ml/2 tbsp chopped fresh parsley

1 bay leaf

Salt and freshly ground black pepper

15 ml/1 tbsp cornflour (cornstarch)

30 ml/2 tbsp water

FOR THE VEGETABLES
1 aubergine (eggplant), diced

1 large red (bell) pepper, diced

1 large green pepper, diced

2 large courgettes (zucchini), diced

2 beefsteak tomatoes, diced

30 ml/2 tbsp tomato purée (paste)

2.5 ml/½ tsp caster (superfine) sugar

2.5 ml/½ tsp dried oregano

1 Fry (sauté) the onion and garlic in 15 ml/1 tbsp of the oil, stirring, for 4 minutes until golden. Add the beef and continue to cook, stirring, until all the grains are separate and no longer pink.

2 Add the stock, wine, herbs and some salt and pepper. Bring to the boil, reduce the heat, part-cover and simmer gently for 20 minutes until the meat is tender. Blend the cornflour with the water and stir into the meat. Bring to the boil and cook for 1 minute, stirring. Taste and re-season, if necessary. Discard the bay leaf.

3 Meanwhile, heat the remaining oil in a separate pan. Add the prepared vegetables, and fry, stirring, for about 2 minutes. Turn down the heat, cover and cook gently for about 10 minutes until tender. Stir in the tomato purée, sugar and oregano and add salt and pepper to taste.

4 Preheat the oven to 190°C/375°F/gas 5/fan oven 170°C.

FOR THE SAUCE

40 g/1½ oz/⅓ cup plain
(all-purpose) flour

600 ml/1 pt/2½ cups milk

1 bouquet garni sachet

25 g/1 oz/2 tbsp butter

TO FINISH

12–16 sheets of no-need-to-precook
lasagne

50 g/2 oz/½ cup freshly grated
Parmesan cheese

FOR THE GARNISH

150 ml/¼ pt/⅔ cup passata (sieved
tomatoes), warmed

A little olive oil

45 ml/3 tbsp chopped fresh parsley

5 Make the sauce. Blend the flour with a little of the milk in a saucepan. Stir in the remaining milk. Add the bouquet garni and butter. Bring to the boil and cook for 2 minutes, stirring all the time. Squeeze the bouquet garni against the sides of the pan to extract all the flavour, then discard. Season the sauce to taste.

6 Spread just enough of the meat mixture to cover the base of a rectangular, 2 litre/3½ pt/8½ cup ovenproof dish. Cover with a layer of lasagne, then half the vegetables, then more lasagne. Add all the remaining meat, then a layer of pasta, followed by the remaining vegetables and finally the last of the pasta. Spoon the sauce over and sprinkle liberally with Parmesan cheese.

7 Bake in the preheated oven for 35–40 minutes until the lasagne is cooked through and the top is golden and the centre feels soft when tested with the point of a knife.

8 Cut the lasagne into six portions. Carefully transfer to the centre of large, warm plates. Drizzle a little passata round the edge of each plate and add a trickle of olive oil. Sprinkle with chopped parsley and serve.

Penne
with pancetta and peas

Tender pasta quills, bathed in a minted cream and onion sauce with diced pancetta and sweet young peas, topped with creamy Mozzarella and a sprinkling of fresh Parmesan cheese.

SERVES 6

500 g/18 oz penne

2 large onions, chopped

50 g/2 oz/¼ cup butter

350 g/12 oz diced pancetta

225 g/8 oz fresh shelled or frozen petit pois

10 ml/2 tsp dried mint

600 ml/1 pt/2½ cups single (light) cream

Salt and freshly ground black pepper

75 g/3 oz/¾ cup grated Mozzarella cheese

45 ml/3 tbsp chopped fresh parsley

75 g/3 oz/¾ cup freshly grated Parmesan cheese

Sprigs of fresh mint, for garnishing

1 Cook the penne in plenty of boiling, lightly salted water according to the packet directions. Drain and return to the pan.

2 Meanwhile, cook the onions gently in the butter in a large saucepan for 2 minutes, stirring until softened but not browned. Add the pancetta and continue to cook for 3 minutes. Add the peas and mint. Turn down the heat very low, cover and cook very gently for 5 minutes, stirring occasionally until the peas are cooked.

3 Tip the pea mixture and the cream into the penne and toss gently over a low heat. Season well and toss again. When hot through, tip into warm pasta bowls.

4 Sprinkle with the Mozzarella, then the parsley and finally the Parmesan. Garnish each with a sprig of mint and serve straight away.

Photograph opposite:
Linguini with Baby Plum Tomatoes in a Chilli Cream Brandy and Amaretto Sauce (see page 66)

Creamy white onion and artichoke risotto
with avocado salad

A traditional, rich risotto made with lightly sautéed white onion, chopped artichoke hearts, fresh chicken stock and dry vermouth, served with a salad of mixed leaves, avocado, black olives and pickled baby silverskin onions.

SERVES 6

120 ml/4 fl oz/½ cup olive oil

3 large white onions, finely chopped

550 g/1¼ lb/2½ cups round-grain (pudding) rice

2 litres/3½ pts/8½ cups hot chicken stock

300 ml/½ pt/1¼ cups dry vermouth

2 x 425 g/15 oz/large cans of artichoke hearts, drained, rinsed and chopped

50 g/2 oz/¼ cup unsalted (sweet) butter

100 g/4 oz/1 cup freshly grated Parmesan cheese

90 ml/6 tbsp crème fraîche

2 avocados

5 ml/1 tsp lemon juice

175 g/6 oz mixed salad leaves

50 g/2 oz black olives

50 g/2 oz pickled baby (pearl) silverskin onions

1 Heat half the oil in a large saucepan. Add the chopped onions and cook gently, stirring, for 2 minutes until softened but not browned.

2 Stir in the rice and cook, stirring, for 1 minute until all the grains are glistening and coated in the oil.

3 Add a quarter of the stock, bring to the boil, reduce the heat and simmer until the liquid has been absorbed. Repeat with a third of the remaining stock. When absorbed, add half the vermouth and simmer again. Add the remaining stock in two batches, allowing each to be absorbed. The risotto should now be creamy but the rice should still have a little 'bite'.

4 Add the last of the vermouth and the artichokes to the risotto and simmer briefly, then stir in the butter, half the cheese and the crème fraîche.

5 Peel, stone (pit) and slice the avocados and toss with the lemon juice to prevent them from going brown.

6 Spoon the risotto on to warm plates. Sprinkle with the remaining cheese. Arrange the salad leaves to one side of each and scatter with the avocado slices, olives and baby onions. Drizzle a little of the remaining olive oil on the salads and around the plates. Serve straight away.

Photograph opposite:
Spiced Chick Pea Croquettes with Roasted Vegetables and Minted Yoghurt Dressing (see page 80)

Three-cheese lasagne verdi
with broccoli and tomatoes

Sheets of green pasta, layered with tiny broccoli florets, chopped tomatoes and Mascarpone, topped with a rich cheese sauce and dusted with Parmesan, then garnished with basil and olives.

SERVES 6

FOR THE SAUCE
40 g/1½ oz/⅓ cup plain (all-purpose) flour
600 ml/1 pt/2½ cups milk
1 large bay leaf
40 g/1½ oz/3 tbsp butter
5 ml/1 tsp made English mustard
100 g/4 oz/1 cup grated Cheddar cheese

FOR THE FILLINGS
350 g/12 oz broccoli, broken into tiny florets
500 g/18 oz/2¼ cups ricotta cheese
75 g/3 oz stoned (pitted) black olives, chopped
2 x 400 g/14 oz/large cans of chopped tomatoes
30 ml/2 tbsp chopped fresh basil
Salt and freshly ground black pepper
30 ml/2 tbsp snipped fresh chives
12–16 sheets of no-need-to-precook lasagne verdi

FOR THE GARNISH
Sprigs of fresh basil
18 black olives

1 Put the flour in a saucepan and add a little of the milk. Blend in, then gradually whisk in the rest of the milk until smooth. Add the bay leaf and butter, bring to the boil and cook for 2 minutes, whisking all the time. Stir in the mustard and Cheddar cheese and season to taste.

2 Cook the broccoli in boiling, lightly salted water for 3–4 minutes until just tender. Drain thoroughly.

3 Preheat the oven to 190°C/375°F/gas 5/fan oven 170°C.

4 Mix the ricotta with the olives and a little salt and pepper.

5 Spread a very thin layer of the sauce into a lightly buttered, rectangular, shallow 2 litre/3½ pt/8½ cup ovenproof dish – you will need to use only about a fifth of it, just enough to moisten the base of the lasagne.

6 Put a layer of lasagne sheets on top, breaking to fit.

7 Cover with half the broccoli and half the chopped tomatoes. Sprinkle over half the basil and a little salt and pepper. Cover with more lasagne, then spread with all the ricotta and scatter over the chives and olives. Add another layer of lasagne, then the remaining broccoli, tomatoes, basil and some salt and pepper. Finally, top with the remaining lasagne and cover with the cheese sauce. Sprinkle liberally with the Parmesan.

8 Bake in the preheated oven for 35–40 minutes until the top is golden brown and the lasagne is cooked through. Test by pushing a sharp pointed knife down through the centre. The lasagne should feel soft.

9 Cut the lasagne into six portions. Carefully transfer to warm plates. Garnish each plate with a sprig of basil and a cluster of three olives and serve.

Chicken and cacciatore pilaf
with crisp sautéed aubergine

A pan-cooked saffron rice dish made with tender chicken thighs, sliced cacciatore sausage and moist and flavoursome whole button mushrooms, garnished with slices of crisply fried aubergine.

SERVES 6

1 aubergine (eggplant), sliced

Salt and freshly ground black pepper

30 ml/2 tbsp olive oil

1 large onion, chopped

2 garlic cloves, crushed

6 chicken thighs, skinned and cut in half

350 g/12 oz/1½ cups long-grain rice

5 ml/1 tsp saffron strands

900 ml/1½ pts/3¾ cups chicken stock

175 g/6 oz baby button mushrooms, left whole

175 g/6 oz cacciatore or chorizo sausage, sliced

200 g/7 oz/1 small can of pimientos, diced

75 g/3 oz frozen peas

5 ml/1 tsp dried oregano

50 g/2 oz/½ cup cornflour (cornstarch)

Corn oil, for shallow-frying

FOR THE GARNISH

1 lemon, cut into wedges

Sprigs of fresh parsley

1 Sprinkle the aubergine slices with salt, place in a colander and leave to stand while making the rest of the dish.

2 Heat the oil in a large, heavy-based shallow pan. Add the onion, garlic and chicken and fry (sauté), stirring and turning the chicken, for 3 minutes. Stir in the rice and saffron.

3 Add the stock and bring to the boil.

4 Add all the remaining ingredients except the aubergine and cornflour. Cover tightly, reduce the heat to as low as possible and simmer for 40 minutes. Stir and check everything is tender and the liquid has been absorbed. The rice should be moist, like a risotto, but soft. If not, re-cover and cook for a further few minutes.

5 When the rice has been cooking for about 25 minutes, rinse the aubergine and pat dry on kitchen paper (paper towels). Season the cornflour with a little salt and pepper. Dip in the aubergine slices to coat completely. Heat the oil for shallow-frying in a large frying pan (skillet) and fry the slices for about 2 minutes on each side until crisp and golden. Drain on kitchen paper.

6 Spoon the pilaf on to warm plates, garnish with the aubergine slices, wedges of lemon and sprigs of fresh parsley and serve.

Café style Saffron, which is the dried stigmas of a type of crocus, is the most expensive spice you can find because it has to be hand-picked. However, I think it is worth the price to give its wonderful colour and aroma to a dish, and fortunately you only need a very tiny quantity. You can use a pinch of ground turmeric to give a similar colour, but the flavour won't be anything like as good!

Baked ham and Gorgonzola risotto
with braised celery

A richly flavoured ham and cheese risotto baked in the oven until tender and creamy, served in a sauce of white wine, garlic and fresh tomatoes and garnished with sticks of braised celery.

SERVES 6

2 large red onions, finely chopped

120 ml/4 fl oz/½ cup olive oil

700 g/1½ lb/3 cups risotto (arborio) rice

2.25 litres/4 pts/10 cups chicken stock

Salt and freshly ground black pepper

350 g/12 oz Gorgonzola cheese, diced

175 g/6 oz piece of smoked ham, diced

60 ml/4 tbsp chopped fresh parsley

1 head of celery, trimmed, reserving the leaves

450 g/1 lb beefsteak tomatoes, skinned and finely chopped

1 garlic clove, crushed

150 ml/¼ pt/⅔ cup dry white wine

2.5 ml/½ tsp caster (superfine) sugar

25 g/1 oz/2 tbsp unsalted (sweet) butter

1 Preheat the oven to 180°C/350°F/gas 4/fan oven 160°C.

2 In a large, flameproof casserole (Dutch oven), fry (sauté) one of the onions in 60 ml/4 tbsp of the olive oil for 2 minutes until softened but not browned.

3 Add the rice and stir until each grain is glistening in oil. Stir in 2 litres/3½ pts/8½ cups of the stock and bring to the boil, stirring all the time. Season with pepper, then add the cheese, ham and half the parsley. Cover.

4 Cut the celery sticks into matchsticks. Put in a separate casserole with the remaining stock. Cover with a lid or foil.

5 Bake the risotto and the celery in the preheated oven for about 30 minutes until the rice has absorbed the liquid and the celery is just tender.

6 Meanwhile, make the sauce. Fry the remaining onion in the remaining oil in a saucepan for 2 minutes until softened but not browned. Add the tomatoes, garlic, wine, sugar and a little salt and pepper. Bring to the boil, reduce the heat, cover and simmer for about 5 minutes until pulpy. Taste and re-season, if necessary.

7 When the risotto is cooked, stir in the butter, taste and re-season. Drain the celery stock into the tomato sauce and stir.

8 Spoon the sauce on to warm plates and pile the risotto in the centre. Arrange the braised celery to one side. Garnish with the celery leaves and sprinkle the risotto with the remaining parsley.

Hints and variations This is also delicious made with diced salami instead of the ham. Cheddar and Gruyère (Swiss) cheese can be substituted for the Gorgonzola, too.

vegetarian main courses

The vibrant colours textures and flavours of Mediterranean vegetables are ideal for meat-free main dishes. They marry well with pulses, cheeses and eggs to form balanced, delicious dishes to tempt the palate of all your friends and family, including even the most dedicated meat-lover. If you are cooking for serious vegetarians, do make sure all the ingredients you use are suitable. Note that some unexpected items, such as Worcestershire sauce, can contain animal products. As with the other main course chapters, you will find everything you need to accompany your vegetarian meal included in each recipe, together with serving suggestions.

Leek and cream cheese tartlets
with a walnut and toasted mustard seed dressing

A delicately flavoured leek and cheese custard, baked in a crisp, golden, flaky shell and served with a dressing made with walnuts and toasted black mustard seeds, enhanced with walnut oil and the zest of an orange.

SERVES 6

450 g/1 lb puff pastry (paste), thawed if frozen

FOR THE FILLING
50 g/2 oz/¼ cup butter

4 leeks, trimmed and thickly sliced

3 eggs

275 g/10 oz/1¼ cups cream cheese

Salt and freshly ground black pepper

15 ml/1 tbsp chopped fresh sage

FOR THE DRESSING
20 ml/1½ tbsp black mustard seeds

75 ml/5 tbsp orange juice

15 ml/1 tbsp lemon juice

5 ml/1 tsp dried minced (ground) onion

120 ml/4 fl oz/½ cup olive oil

45 ml/3 tbsp red wine vinegar

20 ml/1½ tbsp walnut oil

10 ml/2 tsp clear honey

75 g/3 oz/¾ cup walnut halves, finely chopped

1 Preheat the oven to 220°C/425°F/gas 7/fan oven 200°C.

2 Cut the pastry into six equal rectangles. Roll out thinly to 12.5 x 15 cm/5 x 6 in. Score a line in the pastry about 2 cm/¾ in from the outer edge all round to form the rim of each tartlet. Place on two dampened baking (cookie) sheets. Chill for at least 30 minutes.

3 Meanwhile, melt the butter in a saucepan. Add the leeks and fry (sauté), stirring, for 2 minutes until slightly softened. Turn down the heat, cover and cook gently for 4 minutes until fairly soft but still with some shape and not browned. Tip into a bowl and leave to cool.

4 Beat the eggs and use a little to brush round the 'rim' of each pastry case (pie shell). Beat the cheese into the remainder with some salt and pepper and the sage. Stir in the chopped leeks.

5 Spread the mixture in the centre of the pastry rectangles, leaving the rims free.

6 Bake in the preheated oven for 10 minutes, then turn down the heat to 190°C/375°F/gas 5/fan oven 170°C and cook for a further 5 minutes or until the filling is set and the edges are puffy and golden.

7 Meanwhile, make the dressing. Toast the mustard seeds in a frying pan (skillet) until they start to 'pop', then tip them into a bowl. Add all the remaining dressing ingredients except the chopped nuts and whisk well until thick and well blended, then stir in the nuts. Season to taste with salt and pepper.

FOR THE GARNISH
6 small sprigs of fresh sage or parsley

18 walnut halves

8 Transfer the tartlets to warm plates. Spoon some dressing around each one, not quite touching the pastry, and garnish with a cluster of walnuts and a small sprig of sage or parsley.

Serving suggestions New potatoes and a cool, crisp mixed salad will round off this simple but delicious meal.

Hints and variations If you aren't keen on walnuts, use the pesto dressing from page 27 instead.

Café style These look wonderful if you garnish the plates with tomato 'water lilies'. They are quite simple to make. Stand a small, firm tomato on a board, stalk-end down. Make three cross-cuts, no more than 5 mm/¼ in into the flesh, cutting through the skin and outer flesh only, and slicing down towards the base without cutting right through. Gently ease back the points, to resemble petals, leaving the seeds intact in the centre, to represent the stamens.

Spiced chick pea croquettes
with roasted vegetables and minted yoghurt dressing

Crisp, golden, fried rolls made with crushed chick peas, flavoured with cumin, coriander and garlic, served with a selection of colourful Mediterranean vegetables and a cool yoghurt and fresh herb dressing See photograph opposite page 73.

SERVES 6

FOR THE DRESSING
300 ml/½ pt/1¼ cups thick plain yoghurt

30 ml/2 tbsp chopped fresh mint

15 ml/1 tbsp snipped fresh chives

Salt and freshly ground black pepper

FOR THE ROASTED VEGETABLES
2 red (bell) pepper, cut into 6 strips

2 green peppers, cut into 6 strips

2 yellow peppers, cut into 6 strips

2 large courgettes (zucchini), cut into diagonal slices

2 small aubergines (eggplants), cut into diagonal slices

2 red onions, cut into 6 wedges

60 ml/4 tbsp olive oil

1 Preheat the oven at 200°C/400°F/gas 6/fan oven 180°C.

2 Mix the yoghurt with the mint, chives and a little salt and pepper, then cover and chill until ready to serve.

3 Spread all the prepared vegetables out in a roasting tin (pan). Drizzle with the olive oil. Bake in the preheated oven for about 45 minutes, turning once or twice, until tender and slightly charred round the edges.

4 Meanwhile, make the croquettes. Drop the onions into a food processor with the machine running and chop roughly.

5 Add the garlic and chick peas and run the machine until fairly smooth, stopping and scraping down the sides as necessary.

6 Blend in the spices, parsley, potato flour and some salt and pepper.

7 Shape into 18 small rolls. Dip in the plain flour, then the milk, then the flour again, to coat completely. Chill for 15 minutes.

8 Shallow-fry the cakes in hot oil for about 3 minutes, turning once, until crisp and golden. Drain on kitchen paper (paper towels).

9 Spoon the roasted vegetables on to six warm plates. Sprinkle with a little coarse sea salt. Put the croquettes to one side and spoon a little dressing over. Garnish the plates with sprigs of fresh coriander and serve.

Café style You can serve the croquettes on skewers for effect if you wish.

FOR THE CROQUETTES

2 onions, quartered

1 garlic clove, crushed

2 x 425 g/15 oz/large cans of
chick peas (garbanzos), drained

10 ml/2 tsp ground coriander (cilantro)

10 ml/2 tsp ground cumin

30 ml/2 tbsp chopped fresh parsley

30 ml/2 tbsp potato flour

75 g/3 oz/¾ cup plain (all-purpose) flour

90 ml/6 tbsp milk

Corn oil, for shallow-frying

5 ml/1 tsp coarse sea salt

Sprigs of fresh coriander, for garnishing

Serving suggestions Warm, crusty bread tastes wonderful with this. Better still, try a fragrant flavoured variety, such as cheese or rosemary and garlic focaccia. For a contrast of texture, offer a crisp green salad.

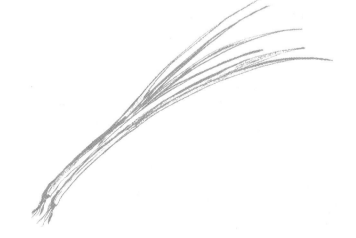

Spinach galettes
with poached egg and creamy onion sauce

Crisp, thin oven-baked spinach and potato cakes, spread with sun-dried tomato and olive oil paste, topped with a poached egg and served with a creamy white onion sauce, garnished with fresh chives.

SERVES 6

900 g/2 lb potatoes

500 g/18 oz baby spinach

1 small onion, grated

50 g/2 oz/½ cup plain (all-purpose) flour

A good pinch of grated nutmeg

Salt and freshly ground black pepper

2 eggs, beaten

100 g/4 oz/1 cup dried breadcrumbs

60 ml/4 tbsp olive oil

FOR THE SAUCE
3 white onions, thinly sliced

450 ml/¾ pt/2 cups milk

25 g/1 oz/2 tbsp butter

150 ml/¼ pt/⅔ cup single (light) cream

1 Preheat the oven to 200°C/400°F/gas 6/fan oven 180°C.

2 Peel and cut the potatoes into small chunks. Boil in lightly salted water until tender. Drain thoroughly, return to the pan and mash well.

3 Wash the spinach well. Cook in a covered pan with no added water for 5 minutes. Drain thoroughly in a colander and press out all the excess water with the back of a spoon.

4 Chop the spinach with scissors, then add to the potatoes with the onion, 15 ml/1 tbsp of the flour, the nutmeg and a little salt and pepper. Beat well.

5 Put the beaten eggs on a plate. Put 20 g/¾ oz/3 tbsp of the remaining flour on a separate plate and the breadcrumbs on a third.

6 With floured hands, shape the mixture until 18 thin, flat cakes. Dip each in flour, then beaten egg, then the breadcrumbs, to coat completely. Transfer to two baking (cookie) sheets, brushed thoroughly with 15 ml/1 tbsp of the oil. Brush the tops with a further 15 ml/1 tbsp of the oil.

7 Bake the cakes in the preheated oven for 25 minutes, swapping the positions of the baking sheets halfway through cooking.

8 Meanwhile, make the sauce. Simmer the white onions in 300 ml/ ½ pt/1¼ cups of the milk in a covered pan for 5 minutes until soft. Stir in 15 g/½ oz/1 tbsp of the butter. Blend the remaining flour with the remaining milk. Stir into the pan and bring to the boil, stirring. Cook for 2 minutes, then stir in the cream and season to taste. Thin with a little extra milk, if necessary, to make a thick pouring sauce.

TO FINISH
6 eggs

45 ml/3 tbsp sun-dried tomato purée (paste)

15 ml/1 tbsp lemon juice (optional)

FOR THE GARNISH
100 g/4 oz cherry tomatoes

A small bunch of fresh chive stalks

9 Mix the tomato purée with the remaining olive oil and a good grinding of black pepper.

10 Poach the eggs in an egg poacher or in water with the lemon juice for 3–5 minutes until cooked to your liking. You can do this either on the hob or in the microwave.

11 Quickly spread the tomato purée on six of the galettes. Place one on each of six warm plates and top each with a poached egg. Arrange two more galettes on each plate and spoon the sauce around.

12 Garnish the plates with a cluster of halved cherry tomatoes and a few chive stalks and serve.

Serving suggestions For a simple but elegant meal, offer some warm, crusty bread and a mixed salad.

Griddled aubergine sandwiches
with tapenade and Mozzarella

Seared slices of aubergine, layered with olives, basil and Mozzarella, baked until the cheese is creamy and melted, then served on couscous with a fresh tomato sauce.

SERVES 6

3 large aubergines (eggplants), trimmed

Salt and freshly ground black pepper

60 ml/4 tbsp olive oil

100 g/4 oz stoned (pitted) black olives

Finely grated zest of ½ lemon

2.5 ml/½ tsp dried oregano

275 g/10 oz Mozzarella cheese, thinly sliced

60 ml/4 tbsp chopped fresh basil

350 g/12 oz/2 cups couscous

900 ml/1½ pts/3¾ cups hot vegetable stock

600 ml/1 pt/2½ cups passata (sieved tomatoes)

2.5 ml/½ tsp garlic salt

5 ml/1 tsp dried basil

Small sprigs of fresh basil, for garnishing

1 Preheat the oven to 190°C/375°F/gas 5/fan oven 170°C.

2 Cut each aubergine lengthways into six slices. Brush the slices on each side with a little of the olive oil. Heat a large griddle pan until very hot, then sear the aubergine slices for 2–3 minutes on each side until lightly cooked and striped brown.

3 Put the olives in a blender or food processor with the lemon zest and oregano. Run the machine and gradually add the remaining olive oil, stopping and scraping down the sides until a rough paste is formed.

4 Spread 12 slices of aubergine with the olive paste. Put six of these slices side by side in a large, lightly oiled baking tin (pan). Top with slices of Mozzarella and a sprinkling of chopped basil. Repeat these layers once, then finish with the plain slices of aubergine. Cover the baking tin with foil and bake in the preheated oven for 15 minutes.

5 Meanwhile, put the couscous in an ovenproof dish. Pour on the hot vegetable stock and stir well. Put near the bottom of the oven for 5 minutes until the stock is absorbed. Remove from the oven and fluff up with a fork.

6 Put the passata, garlic salt and basil in a saucepan and heat through.

7 Spoon the couscous on warm plates. Top with the aubergine stacks. Trickle a little sauce over (don't smother the aubergine) and a little more round the edge of the plate. Garnish each with a small sprig of basil and serve.

Serving suggestions Offer a basket of warm ciabatta bread and a crisp green salad.

Café style When spooning out the couscous, don't try to be too neat – allow a few grains to fall to the side of each mound.

Spring vegetable ragoût
with goats' cheese crostini

A mélange of white beans, baby carrots, potatoes, corn cobs, turnips, leeks and okra, in a rich sauce, topped with slices of toasted French bread, smothered in soft goats' cheese.

SERVES 6

225 g/8 oz/1⅓ cups haricot (navy) beans, soaked in cold water for several hours or overnight

50 g/2 oz/¼ cup butter

1 large onion, chopped

18 baby waxy potatoes, scrubbed

3 baby turnips, quartered

175 g/6 oz baby carrots, scrubbed, topped and tailed

100 g/4 oz baby corn cobs

2 leeks, sliced

900 ml/1½ pts/3¾ cups vegetable stock

400 g/14 oz/1 large can of chopped tomatoes

15 ml/1 tbsp brandy

1 bay leaf

Salt and freshly ground black pepper

225 g/8 oz okra (ladies' fingers)

1 large carrot

12 slices of French bread

120 g/4½ oz soft goats' cheese

30 ml/2 tbsp chopped fresh parsley

6 sprigs of fresh parsley, for garnishing

1 Drain the soaked beans and place in a large saucepan. Cover with cold water. Bring to the boil and boil rapidly for 10 minutes, then reduce the heat, part-cover and simmer for about 1 hour until the beans are tender. Drain.

2 Melt half the butter in the saucepan. Add the onion and fry (sauté) for 2 minutes, stirring. Add the beans, potatoes, the baby vegetables and the leeks, stock, tomatoes, brandy, bay leaf and some salt and pepper. Bring to the boil, reduce the heat and simmer for 15 minutes.

3 Add the okra and simmer for a further 15 minutes, stirring occasionally, until all the vegetables are tender and bathed in a rich sauce. Boil rapidly for a few minutes to reduce the liquid slightly if necessary.

4 Meanwhile, shave off strips of the large carrot lengthways with a potato peeler. Blanch in boiling water for 2 minutes. Drain, rinse with cold water and drain again. Roll up to form rosettes.

5 Toast the French bread on one side. Spread the untoasted sides with the remaining butter, then the goats' cheese. Return to the grill (broiler) until melted and bubbling.

6 Discard the bay leaf from the vegetables. Taste and re-season, if necessary. Ladle into warm bowls and top each with two cheese toasts. Seat each bowl on a large plate, put a sprig of parsley to one side of the bowl with a few rosettes of carrot and serve.

Serving suggestions This is a delicious, filling meal in itself, but you could offer a fresh, cool salad, such as mixed green leaves or sliced tomatoes with onion rings, as an accompaniment.

Parsnip and walnut soufflé pie
with courgette relish

A fluffy, golden parsnip and walnut soufflé in a crisp cheese pastry case, served with a sweet, spicy relish of shredded courgettes, spring onion, cucumber and raisins in honey and sherry vinegar.

SERVES 6

FOR THE RELISH
15 ml/1 tbsp olive oil

1 large courgette (zucchini), cut into very thin matchsticks

1 bunch of spring onions (scallions), chopped

10 cm/4 in piece of cucumber, cut into very thin matchsticks

50 g/2 oz/$\frac{1}{3}$ cup raisins

40 ml/2$\frac{1}{2}$ tbsp clear honey

60 ml/4 tbsp sherry vinegar

2.5 ml/$\frac{1}{2}$ tsp mixed (apple-pie) spice

2.5 ml/$\frac{1}{2}$ tsp chilli powder

Salt and freshly ground black pepper

FOR THE PASTRY (PASTE)
350 g/12 oz/3 cups plain (all-purpose) flour

1.5 ml/$\frac{1}{4}$ tsp ground cinnamon

75 g/3 oz/$\frac{1}{3}$ cup butter

75 g/3 oz/$\frac{1}{3}$ cup white vegetable fat

100 g/4 oz/1 cup grated strong Cheddar cheese

2 eggs, separated

75 ml/5 tbsp cold water

1 To make the relish, heat the oil in a saucepan. Add the prepared vegetables and raisins and stir until they are all coated in the oil. Add the honey, vinegar and spices and cook for 3 minutes, stirring gently, until a thick relish is formed but the vegetables are still holding their shape. Remove from the heat.

2 Make the pastry. Sift the flour, cinnamon and a good pinch of salt into a large bowl. Cut 75 g/3 oz/$\frac{1}{3}$ cup of the butter and all the white fat into pieces, add to the bowl and rub in with your fingertips until the mixture resembles breadcrumbs. Stir in the grated cheese. Mix the two egg yolks with the water and stir into the mixture to bind. (Reserve the whites for the filling.)

3 Knead the pastry gently on a lightly floured surface, then wrap in clingfilm (plastic wrap) and chill while preparing the filling.

4 Preheat the oven to 200°C/400°F/gas 6/fan oven 180°C.

5 Cook the parsnips in boiling, lightly salted water for about 10 minutes or until tender. Drain thoroughly and mash with the butter and the milk. Stir in the walnuts and the three egg yolks and season with salt and pepper.

6 Roll out the pastry and use to line two 18 cm/7 in flan dishes (pie pans). Prick the bases with a fork. Fill with crumpled foil and bake in the preheated oven for 10 minutes. Remove the foil and return the flans to the oven for 5 minutes to dry out.

7 Whisk all five egg whites until stiff. Beat 30 ml/2 tbsp into the parsnip mixture to slacken it, then fold in the remainder with a metal spoon. Turn into the pastry cases (pie shells). Bake in the oven for 25 minutes until risen and golden brown. Meanwhile, reheat the relish.

FOR THE FILLING

700 g/1½ lb parsnips, cut into chunks

75 g/3 oz/⅓ cup butter

120 ml/4 fl oz/½ cup milk

175 g/6 oz/1½ cups walnuts, finely chopped

3 eggs, separated

FOR THE GARNISH

Mixed salad leaves

Sliced radishes

8 Cut each flan into six wedges. Arrange two wedges on each of six warm plates. Put a spoonful of the relish to one side. Garnish the plates with salad leaves and radish slices and serve.

Serving suggestions These go perfectly with jacket potatoes and French (green) beans. Cut a cross in the top of each baked potato and squeeze gently to open. Top with soured (dairy sour) cream and snipped fresh chives.

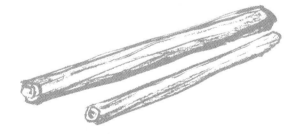

Marinated tofu and mixed vegetable beignets
with aioli

Cubes of firm tofu marinated in a tangy mixture of olive oil, lemon juice, ground cumin and fresh coriander, with deep-fried button mushrooms, sweet potatoes and baby courgettes, all served with a creamy garlic mayonnaise.

SERVES 6

2 x 250 g/9 oz blocks of firm tofu

1 small onion, finely chopped

Finely grated zest and juice of 1 lemon

40 ml/2½ tbsp olive oil

5 ml/1 tsp ground cumin

30 ml/2 tbsp chopped fresh coriander (cilantro)

Salt and freshly ground black pepper

1 sweet potato, cut into slices

24 baby courgettes (zucchini)

225 g/8 oz/2 cups plain (all-purpose) flour

175 ml/6 fl oz/¾ cup lukewarm water

450 ml/¾ pt/2 cups mayonnaise

3 garlic cloves, crushed

A few drops of Tabasco sauce

2 egg whites

24 button mushrooms

Corn oil, for deep-frying

FOR THE GARNISH
6 sprigs of fresh coriander

Wedges of lemon

1 Drain the tofu and cut into 1 cm/½ in dice. Place in a bowl with the onion, lemon zest and all but 5 ml/1 tsp of the juice. Add 30 ml/2 tbsp of the olive oil, the cumin, coriander, 5 ml/1 tsp of salt and a good grinding of pepper. Mix well and leave to marinate for at least 1 hour.

2 Blanch the sweet potato slices and courgettes for 3 minutes in boiling water. Drain and dry on kitchen paper (paper towels).

3 Mix the flour with 5 ml/1 tsp of salt in a bowl. Gradually add the water to form a thick, smooth batter. Whisk the egg whites until stiff and fold into the batter with a metal spoon.

4 Mix the mayonnaise with the garlic, the remaining lemon juice, the Tabasco and a good grinding of black pepper. Spoon into six little pots.

5 Drain the tofu and pat dry on kitchen paper (paper towels).

6 Heat the oil for deep-frying to 190°C/375°F or until a cube of day-old bread browns in 30 seconds.

7 Dip each piece of tofu in the batter and deep-fry for 3–4 minutes in batches until golden brown and cooked through. Repeat with the vegetables. Keep each batch separate so you know which ingredient is which. Drain on kitchen paper.

8 Pile a selection of the beignets on warm plates with a small pot of aioli on each plate. Garnish with coriander and wedges of lemon and serve hot.

Serving suggestions These hot golden treats are complemented particularly well with a tomato and avocado salad. I offer a basket of warm crusty bread, too, for those guests with large appetites!

Potato gnocchi
with Dolcelatte sauce and glazed roasted vine tomatoes

Freshly made potato gnocchi smothered in a smooth crème fraîche sauce, richly flavoured with blue cheese, and garnished with sprigs of small, sweet, red tomatoes, glazed in olive oil and balsamic vinegar.

SERVES 6

700 g/1½ lb potatoes, cut into small pieces

Freshly ground black pepper

1.5 ml/¼ tsp celery salt

1 large egg, beaten

175 g/6 oz/1½ cups plain (all-purpose) flour

450 ml/¾ pt/2 cups crème fraîche

175 g/6 oz Dolcelatte cheese, cut into small pieces

15 ml/1 tbsp snipped fresh chives

50 g/2 oz piece of fresh Parmesan cheese

6 sprigs of small red tomatoes, on the vine

60 ml/4 tbsp olive oil

10 ml/2 tsp caster (superfine) sugar

30 ml/2 tbsp balsamic vinegar

A few whole chive stalks, for garnishing

1 Preheat the oven to 200°C/400°F/gas 6/fan oven 180°C.

2 Cook the potatoes in boiling water until very soft. Drain and return to the pan over a gentle heat for a few moments to dry out.

3 Mash the potatoes thoroughly, then add a good grinding of pepper, the celery salt and egg. Mix well, then work in enough flour to form a soft but not sticky dough. With floured hands, shape the mixture into 36 small ovals.

4 Bring a large pan of water to the boil. Drop in nine of the gnocchi at a time and cook for 3 minutes until they all float to the surface. Remove with a draining spoon and drain on kitchen paper (paper towels). Repeat with the remaining gnocchi.

5 Place the gnocchi in six small buttered shallow ovenproof dishes (or one large one if you prefer). Mix the crème fraîche with the Dolcelatte and the chives. Grate half the Parmesan and add this to the sauce, then spoon the sauce over the gnocchi. Bake in the preheated oven for about 25 minutes or until golden brown and bubbling.

6 Lay the sprigs of tomatoes in a roasting tin (pan). Whisk the olive oil, sugar and balsamic vinegar together and pour over the fruit. Bake at the top of the oven for 10 minutes until just soft but still holding their shape. Shave the remaining Parmesan.

7 Put each individual dish of gnocchi on a warm plate. If you have made one large dish, spoon a portion of gnocchi on to each plate. Scatter the Parmesan shavings over, lay a sprig of tomatoes to one side of each and spoon over the pan juices. Add a few chives stalks for garnish and serve.

Serving suggestions Keep it simple – hot plain or garlic ciabatta bread and a crisp green salad are all this needs.

Tomato and onion gougère
with Swiss cheese fondue

Fresh tomatoes and onions, baked in a light, golden, choux pastry case, and presented with a velvety cheese sauce, flavoured with garlic, kirsch and dry white wine, then garnished with tomato water lillies.

SERVES 6

FOR THE PASTRY (PASTE)
150 g/5 oz/1¼ cups plain (all-purpose) flour

A good pinch of salt

300 ml/½ pt/1¼ cups water

50 g/2 oz/¼ cup butter

4 eggs, beaten

25 g/1 oz/¼ cup grated Cheddar cheese

FOR THE FILLING
50 g/2 oz/¼ cup butter

4 large onions, sliced

6 beefsteak tomatoes, skinned and chopped

5 ml/1 tsp dried basil

5 ml/1 tsp caster (superfine) sugar

15 ml/1 tbsp tomato purée (paste)

1 Preheat the oven to 220°C/425°F/gas 7/fan oven 200°C.

2 Sift the flour and salt on to a sheet of kitchen paper (paper towel). Put the water and butter in a saucepan. Heat gently until the butter melts, then bring to the boil. Add the flour all at once and beat with a wooden spoon until the mixture leaves the sides of the pan clean. Remove from the heat.

3 Add the beaten eggs a little at a time, beating well after each addition until smooth and glossy but the mixture still holds its shape.

4 Spoon the mixture round the edge of a greased, large, rectangular 2 litre/3½ pt/8½ cup baking dish. Sprinkle with the Cheddar cheese.

5 Make the filling. Melt the butter in a saucepan. Add the onions and cook, stirring, for 2 minutes. Add the tomatoes, basil, sugar and a little salt and pepper. Cover and cook gently for 5 minutes. Remove the lid and continue cooking for a few minutes until pulpy, stirring occasionally. Taste and re-season, if necessary.

6 Spoon the mixture into the centre of the choux pastry case (shell). Bake in the preheated oven for 30 minutes until risen and golden.

7 Meanwhile, make the fondue. Rub the cut garlic clove round the inside of a saucepan and discard. Blend the cornflour and water in the pan. Add the wine, kirsch, lemon juice, both the cheeses, the nutmeg and a good grinding of pepper. Heat gently, stirring all the time, until thick and creamy.

8 Using a sharp knife, cut each cherry tomato into a water lily (see page 79).

FOR THE FONDUE

1 garlic clove, halved

15 ml/1 tbsp cornflour (cornstarch)

15 ml/1 tbsp water

300 ml/½ pt/1¼ cups dry white wine

30 ml/2 tbsp kirsch

5 ml/1 tsp lemon juice

200 g/7 oz/1¾ cups grated
Cheddar cheese

225 g/8 oz/2 cups grated Gruyère
(Swiss) cheese

A good pinch of grated nutmeg

FOR THE GARNISH

6 cherry tomatoes

A few mixed salad leaves

9 Cut the gougère into six pieces. Transfer to large warm plates. Trickle a little fondue over the filling and around the gougère. Arrange a tomato flower and a few salad leaves to one side and serve.

Serving suggestions Some hot French bread will help to mop up the fondue, and a crisp mixed leaf salad makes a refreshing accompaniment.

Hints and variations Ring the changes by using 225 g/8 oz of sliced button mushrooms and 2 sliced leeks instead of the onions.

Watercress and mushroom roulade
with Hollandaise sauce

A light, fluffy roulade made with watercress, parsley and freshly grated Parmesan, filled with button mushrooms and sun-dried tomatoes, served with a fresh, buttery Hollandaise sauce.

SERVES 6

FOR THE FILLING

50 g/2 oz/¼ cup butter

15 ml/1 tbsp oil from a jar of sun-dried tomatoes

1 large onion, finely chopped

100 g/4 oz button mushrooms, sliced

2 sun-dried tomatoes in olive oil, chopped

400 g/14 oz/1 large can of chopped tomatoes

5 ml/1 tsp caster (superfine) sugar

Salt and freshly ground black pepper

FOR THE ROULADE

2 bunches of watercress

30 ml/2 tbsp chopped fresh parsley

150 g/5 oz/1¼ cups freshly grated Parmesan cheese

8 eggs, separated

1 Grease two 18 x 28 cm/7 x 11 in Swiss roll tins (jelly roll pans). Line with oiled greaseproof (waxed) paper.

2 Make the filling. Heat the butter and sun-dried tomato oil in a saucepan. Add the onion and mushrooms and cook, stirring, for 2 minutes until softened but not browned.

3 Add the sun-dried and canned tomatoes, the sugar and a little salt and pepper. Boil rapidly for about 8 minutes until pulpy.

4 Preheat the oven to 200°C/400°F/gas 6/fan oven 180°C.

5 Meanwhile, trim off the feathery ends of the watercress stalks, then reserve six sprigs for garnishing and chop the remainder finely. Stir in the parsley, 100 g/4 oz/1 cup of the cheese, the egg yolks and a little salt and pepper.

6 Whisk the egg whites until stiff and fold into the mixture with a metal spoon. Turn into the prepared tins, level the surfaces and bake, one above the other, in the preheated oven for about 10 minutes until golden and firm to the touch.

7 Put two clean sheets of greaseproof paper on the work surface and dust with the remaining Parmesan. Turn the roulades out on to the paper. Using a knife, gently ease off the cooking paper.

8 Reheat the filling. Spread over the roulades and roll up from a short end, using the paper to help you. Once rolled, wrap in the greaseproof paper and return to a low oven to keep warm while you make the sauce.

9 Whisk the eggs and lemon juice in a small saucepan. Gradually whisk in the melted butter. Cook over a very gentle heat, whisking all the time until thickened. Do not allow the mixture to boil or it will curdle. Season the sauce with salt, white pepper and the cayenne.

FOR THE SAUCE

3 eggs

45 ml/3 tbsp lemon juice

175 g/6 oz/¾ cup unsalted (sweet) butter, melted

White pepper

A good pinch of cayenne

10 Slice the roulades, arrange attractively on warm plates and spoon the sauce around. Garnish with the reserved sprigs of watercress and serve.

Serving suggestions Either buttered pasta or new potatoes will go well with this, with some mangetout (snow peas) and baby corn cobs for added colour.

Hints and variations Instead of watercress, you can use 450 g/1 lb of spinach, cooked with no extra water for 5 minutes, then drained very thoroughly and chopped.

Café style Sun-dried tomatoes have an intense, sweet flavour that adds a far more distinctive taste to a dish than their fresh or canned counterparts. Traditionally, the tomatoes were spread out to dry in the hot sun – but today's commercially produced varieties are dried in slow ovens. You can buy them dry in packets, and then soak them before use. Alternatively, they are sold in jars, steeped in olive oil. The soaking water or oil may be used in cooking to give added flavour.

Vegetable summer pudding
with Mascarpone and warm white bean salad

A medley of Mediterranean vegetables and tomatoes, pressed into a bread-lined mould, then sliced and served with cool Mascarpone cheese and warm cannellini beans, dressed with extra-virgin olive oil and freshly ground black pepper.

VEGETARIAN MAIN COURSES

SERVES 6

120 ml/4 fl oz/¹/₂ cup extra-virgin olive oil

1 onion, finely chopped

1 red (bell) pepper, finely chopped

1 large carrot, coarsely grated

1 large turnip, coarsely grated

2 courgettes (zucchini), coarsely grated

450 g/1 lb ripe beefsteak tomatoes, skinned and roughly chopped

5 ml/1 tsp herbes de Provence

Salt and freshly ground black pepper

A good pinch of caster (superfine) sugar

8 large slices of white or wholemeal bread, crusts removed

225 g/8 oz/1¹/₃ cups dried cannellini beans

45 ml/3 tbsp chopped fresh parsley

250 g/9 oz/generous 1 cup Mascarpone cheese

FOR THE GARNISH
18 black olives

Sprigs of fresh parsley

1 This recipe must be started the day before you intend to serve the pudding. Heat 30 ml/2 tbsp of the oil in a saucepan. Add the prepared vegetables, the tomatoes, herbs, a little salt and pepper and the sugar. Cook, stirring, for 1 minute, then reduce the heat, cover and cook gently for 10 minutes. Taste and re-season, if necessary.

2 Meanwhile, oil a 1.2 litre/2 pt/5 cup pudding basin and line with six of the slices of bread, cutting them to fit tightly together.

3 Spoon the cooked vegetables into the dish. Cover with the remaining slices of bread, cutting them to fit. Cover with greaseproof (waxed) paper, then place a saucer, rounded side down, on top. Weigh down with heavy weights or cans of food.

4 Leave the pudding to cool, then chill overnight. At the same time, put the beans in plenty of cold water to soak overnight.

5 The following day, drain the beans, place in a saucepan and cover with cold water. Bring to the boil and boil rapidly for 10 minutes, then reduce the heat and simmer for about 45 minutes or until tender. Add a good pinch of salt, leave for a few minutes, then drain and return to the saucepan. Add 60 ml/4 tbsp of the remaining oil, and season well with black pepper. Finally, stir in the chopped parsley.

6 Uncover the pudding, loosen the edge with a round-bladed knife and turn out. Cut into six wedges and carefully transfer them to plates. Neaten any filling that spills out with a knife. Spoon the warm beans to the side. Put a generous spoonful of Mascarpone by the pudding and garnish the plates with a few black olives and a sprig of parsley. Finally, trickle any remaining olive oil around.

Serving suggestion This really needs no accompaniment, but you could offer a crisp green salad as well.

Café style The herbes de Provence give this dish a particularly distinctive French Mediterranean flavour. The mixture is a blend of five dried herbs – bay leaves, parsley, sage, thyme and rosemary. As an alternative, use Mediterranean mixed dried herbs – a similar combination that incorporates oregano instead of rosemary.

Vegetable terrine
with a creamy tomato dressing

A soft cheese mousse, set around asparagus, baby carrots and peppers, then sliced and served on a bed of crisp salad, drizzled with a creamy tomato dressing with just a hint of Tabasco.

SERVES 6

175 g/6 oz baby carrots, scraped

100 g/4 oz small thin asparagus spears

2 red (bell) peppers, cut into thin strips

30 ml/2 tbsp/2 sachets of powdered gelatine

100 ml/3½ fl oz/scant ½ cup dry cider

50 g/2 oz/½ cup plain (all-purpose) flour

300 ml/½ pt/1¼ cups milk

40 g/1½ oz/3 tbsp unsalted (sweet) butter

5 ml/1 tsp dried basil

Salt and freshly ground black pepper

3 eggs, separated

700 g/1½ lb/3 cups ricotta cheese

150 ml/¼ pt/⅔ cup double (heavy) cream

15 ml/1 tbsp lemon juice

1 Oil a 1.5 litre/2½ pt/6 cup terrine or loaf tin (pan) and line the base with non-stick baking parchment.

2 Put the carrots in a pan of lightly salted water. Put the asparagus and peppers in a steamer or metal colander that fits on the saucepan. Cover and cook for 5–10 minutes or until the asparagus and peppers are very tender. Remove the steamer and continue to cook the carrots for a further few minutes, if necessary, until soft. Drain the carrots, rinse with cold water and leave all the vegetables to cool.

3 Sprinkle the gelatine over the cider in a small bowl. Leave to soften for 5 minutes, then either stand the bowl in a pan of hot water or heat briefly in the microwave until the gelatine is completely dissolved. Do not allow it to boil.

4 Mix the flour and milk in a saucepan until well blended. Add the butter and basil. Bring to the boil and cook for 2 minutes, stirring all the time until thick and smooth, then season with salt and pepper.

5 Remove from the heat and beat in the egg yolks and the cheese. Stir in the dissolved gelatine.

6 Whisk the egg whites until stiff. Whip the cream and the lemon juice until softly peaking. Fold the cream, then egg whites into the cheese mixture. Taste and add more seasoning, if necessary.

7 Spoon a quarter of the cheese mixture into the prepared terrine or tin. Arrange the carrots over in a single layer. Add a third of the remaining mixture, then lay the asparagus spears on top, pointing in alternate directions. Spoon half the remaining cheese mixture on top, then lay the pepper strips on top and finish with the rest of the cheese mixture. Gently level the surface. Chill until set.

Photograph opposite:
Chicken Avocado and Mango Salad in a Spiced Mayonnaise (see page 106)

FOR THE DRESSING

150 ml/¼ pt/⅔ cup mayonnaise

75 ml/5 tbsp crème fraîche

30 ml/2 tbsp tomato purée (paste)

A few drops of Tabasco sauce

15 ml/1 tbsp Worcestershire sauce

A little milk

FOR THE SALAD

1 curly endive (frisée lettuce)

1 bunch of watercress

8 Whisk all the ingredients for the dressing together. Thin to a pouring consistency with milk and season to taste.

9 Trim the curly endive and watercress. Tear the endive into pieces.

10 Loosen the edges of the terrine all round and turn out on to a board. Cut into 12 slices.

11 Place two slices on each of six plates. Arrange the watercress and endive attractively together to one side and drizzle the tomato dressing over and around. No other garnish is necessary. Serve cold.

Serving suggestions You need no more than some buttered new potatoes to complete this dish perfectly, but you could also serve a tomato and onion salad if you wish.

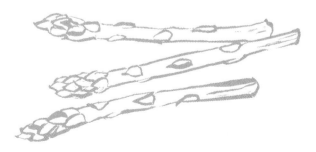

Photograph opposite:
Crème Brûlée with Mango and Passion Fruit (see page 116)

Spiced soya bean and vegetable terrine
with carrot and coriander sauce

Slices of a coarse soya bean and root vegetable terrine, baked in vine leaves and served with a smooth, creamy golden carrot sauce, flavoured with nutmeg and fresh coriander leaves.

SERVES 6

FOR THE TERRINE
225 g/8 oz/1⅓ cups dried soya beans, soaked in cold water for several hours or overnight

50 g/2 oz/¼ cup butter, plus extra for greasing

6 fresh or preserved vine leaves

2 leeks, chopped

1 small parsnip, coarsely grated

1 turnip, coarsely grated

1 potato, coarsely grated

30 ml/2 tbsp mild curry paste

50 g/2 oz/1 cup fresh wholemeal breadcrumbs

30 ml/2 tbsp tomato relish

Salt and freshly ground black pepper

2 eggs, beaten

FOR THE SAUCE
3 large carrots, sliced

50 g/2 oz/¼ cup butter

A pinch of grated nutmeg

30 ml/2 tbsp chopped fresh coriander (cilantro)

90 ml/6 tbsp single (light) cream

Sprigs of fresh coriander, for garnishing

1 Preheat the oven to 190°C/375°F/gas 5/fan oven 170°C.

2 Drain the beans, place in a saucepan and cover with cold water. Bring to the boil and boil rapidly for 10 minutes, then reduce the heat, part-cover and simmer gently for 2–3 hours or until tender, topping up with boiling water as necessary. Drain and mash roughly.

3 Meanwhile, butter a 1 kg/2¼ lb loaf tin (pan) and line with the vine leaves, leaving them overhanging the edges all round. If you use fresh vine leaves, blanch them first for 2 minutes in boiling water.

4 Heat the measured butter in a large saucepan. Add the prepared vegetables and fry (sauté), stirring, for 1 minute. Turn down the heat, cover and cook very gently for 10 minutes, stirring occasionally, until softened but not browned.

5 Remove from the heat, stir in the curry paste, breadcrumbs, relish and mashed beans. Season to taste and stir in the eggs.

6 Turn into the prepared tin and fold the ends of the vine leaves over the top of the loaf. Cover with foil and bake in the preheated oven for 1½ hours until firm.

7 Meanwhile, make the sauce. Cook the carrots in boiling, lightly salted water for about 6 minutes or until tender. Drain and place in a blender or food processor with the remaining ingredients. Purée, then return to the saucepan. Season to taste and reheat.

8 Turn the terrine out and cut into thick slices. Place on warm plates and spoon the sauce around. Garnish with sprigs of coriander and serve.

Serving suggestions Set the slices on a bed of wild rice and add the sauce and garnish, then serve with a tomato and onion salad.

main course salads

We all have a colourful array of salad stuffs now available in our supermarkets and with clever combinations of warm and cold, cooked and raw ingredients, they take on a whole new dimension. Some of the recipes here are traditional European favourites, others have come from further afield to become equally well known, such as Caesar Salad from Mexico – although this one, in particular, could be argued to have Spanish/Mediterranean influences! All the recipes – even the traditional ones – have interesting new twists to make them special and innovative with flavours and textures to tickle the taste buds, and they are all complete meals: warm fresh bread is the only accompaniment you need.

Rustic mixed fried cheese salad
with caper, sun-dried tomato and olive vinaigrette

*Mozzarella, goats' and Fontina cheeses, coated with polenta and fried in olive oil,
served on a bed of tomatoes, peppers, cucumber, baby leaf spinach, red onions and
artichoke hearts, dressed with a vinaigrette.*

SERVES 6

100 g/4 oz/²⁄₃ cup polenta

5 ml/1 tsp dried oregano

350 g/12 oz Fontina cheese

3 x 125 g/4½ oz fresh Mozzarella
cheeses, drained

6 x 70 g/2½ oz individually wrapped
discs of goats' cheese

FOR THE SALAD

6 beefsteak tomatoes, diced

3 Romano peppers, diced

125 g/4½ oz baby leaf spinach

2 red onions, finely chopped

425 g/15 oz/1 large can of artichoke
hearts, drained and quartered

45 ml/3 tbsp extra-virgin olive oil

15 ml/1 tbsp lemon juice

FOR THE DRESSING

30 ml/2 tbsp balsamic vinegar

75 ml/5 tbsp extra-virgin olive oil

Salt and freshly ground black pepper

30 ml/2 tbsp capers, drained

50 g/2 oz stoned (pitted) black olives,
roughly chopped

30 ml/2 tbsp chopped fresh basil

30 ml/2 tbsp chopped fresh parsley

15 ml/1 tbsp snipped fresh chives

2 sun-dried tomatoes in oil, drained and
finely chopped

Olive and sunflower oil, for shallow-frying

1 Mix the polenta with the oregano. Cut the Fontina cheese into six thick fingers. Cut each ball of Mozzarella in half. Dip each piece of cheese in the polenta to coat completely. Chill until ready to cook.

2 Put all the salad ingredients in a large bowl. Toss gently and pile on six large plates.

3 Mix all the dressing ingredients together and season with lots of black pepper.

4 Pour a mixture of olive and sunflower oil to a depth of about 5 mm/¼ in in a large frying pan (skillet) and heat. Fry (sauté) the cheese pieces for about 1 minute on each side until crisp and golden. Drain on kitchen paper (paper towels).

5 Pile on top of the salads and spoon a little dressing over, drizzling the rest around the plates. Serve straight away.

Hints and variations If you can't get Fontina cheese, Gouda works well too.

Mixed prosciutto salad
with conchiglie, Mozzarella, baby plum tomatoes and fresh basil

A selection of the finest cured meats arranged on a platter with a Mozzarella and tomato pasta salad, dressed simply with extra-virgin olive oil, freshly ground black pepper and fragrant fresh basil – a triumph of understatement!

SERVES 6

350 g/12 oz conchiglie (pasta shells)

60 ml/4 tbsp extra-virgin olive oil, plus extra for drizzling

24 baby balls of Mozzarella cheese

18 baby plum tomatoes, halved

1 small bunch of fresh basil

Freshly ground black pepper

450 g/1 lb mixed prosciutto (salami Milano, speck, Parma ham, bresaola, mortadella, etc.)

TO FINISH

75 g/3 oz black olives

Olive oil

Wedges of lemon

1 Cook the pasta according to the packet directions until just al dente. Drain, rinse with cold water and drain again. Tip into a large bowl and add the olive oil. Toss to coat.

2 Add the Mozzarella balls and the halved tomatoes. Pluck off the tiny top sprigs from the basil and reserve. Tear the remainder of the leaves into small pieces. Add to the pasta with lots of freshly ground black pepper. Toss gently.

3 Arrange the meats attractively on six very large plates, leaving room for the salad to one side. Pile the salad to one side and tuck two or three tiny sprigs of fresh basil into each one. Add a few olives and drizzle a little olive oil over the meats. Add a wedge of lemon to each plate and serve.

Café style Always try to use the best-quality, fresh buffalo-milk Mozzarella – the flavour and texture are just divine! Look out for smoked Mozzarella too – a golden, smooth-textured cheese that is delicious nibbled on its own or served with bread.

Café-style Caesar salad
in an egg and anchovy dressing

*Crisp cos lettuce, smoked lardons, sunflower seeds and golden garlic croûtons,
tossed with a creamy coddled egg and anchovy dressing and scattered with
Parmesan shavings and chopped parsley.*

SERVES 6

FOR THE CROÛTONS
6 thick slices of French bread, cut into small cubes

45 ml/3 tbsp olive oil

1 large garlic clove, crushed

A good pinch of cayenne

FOR THE SALAD
225 g/8 oz smoked lardons

2 cos (romaine) lettuces, cut into chunky shreds

50 g/2 oz/½ cup sunflower seeds

FOR THE DRESSING
1 garlic clove, crushed

6 canned anchovy fillets, drained and chopped

120 ml/4 fl oz/½ cup sunflower oil

90 ml/6 tbsp white wine vinegar

15 ml/1 tbsp Dijon mustard

5 ml/1 tsp caster (superfine) sugar

25 g/1 oz/¼ cup freshly grated Parmesan cheese

3 large eggs

Salt and freshly ground black pepper

TO FINISH
25 g/1 oz/¼ cup freshly shaved Parmesan cheese

45 ml/3 tbsp chopped fresh parsley

18 chive stalks

1 Preheat the oven to 220°C/425°F/gas 7/fan oven 200°C.

2 Prepare the croûtons. Mix the bread with the olive oil, garlic and cayenne. Toss until well coated. Spread out on a baking (cookie) sheet.

3 Spread the lardons on another baking sheet. Put the lardons at the top of the oven with the bread just underneath and bake in the preheated oven for about 10 minutes until golden.

4 Divide the lettuce between six large serving bowls. Scatter the sunflower seeds over.

5 Make the dressing. Mash the garlic with the chopped anchovies until they form a paste. Gradually whisk in the sunflower oil, vinegar, mustard, sugar and grated Parmesan.

6 Boil the eggs for 1½ minutes only. Drain and plunge into cold water, then remove the shells and add the eggs to the dressing. Whisk well until thoroughly mixed. Season to taste with salt and pepper.

7 Spoon the creamy dressing over the salads, then scatter with the croûtons and lardons. Finally, sprinkle with the shavings of Parmesan and the chopped parsley and lay three chive stalks over the top of each before serving.

Hints and variations This is also delicious made with strips of smoked chicken instead of the lardons.

You can freeze the remaining anchovies. They will keep for 2–3 months.

Smoked chicken and bulghar salad
with tomato and olive dressing

*Tender morsels of smoked chicken tossed with a selection of crunchy salad stuffs
and fluffy bulghar wheat, in a chunky, colourful dressing of chopped cherry tomatoes,
green and black olives, balsamic vinegar and extra-virgin olive oil.*

SERVES 6

350 g/12 oz/3 cups bulghar
(cracked wheat)

5 ml/1 tsp salt

750 ml/1¼ pts/3 cups boiling water

175 g/6 oz fresh shelled or cooked
frozen peas

75 g/3 oz/½ cup raisins

3 sticks of celery, chopped

1 bunch of spring onions (scallions),
trimmed and chopped

1 green chilli, seeded and
finely chopped

60 ml/4 tbsp extra-virgin olive oil

30 ml/2 tbsp white wine vinegar

Finely grated zest and juice of ½ lime

Freshly ground black pepper

350 g/12 oz smoked chicken breast,
cut into neat pieces

FOR THE DRESSING

75 g/3 oz stoned (pitted) black olives

75 g/3 oz pimiento-stuffed green olives

12 cherry tomatoes, chopped

175 ml/6 fl oz/¾ cup extra-virgin olive oil

90 ml/6 tbsp balsamic vinegar

1 Put the bulghar in a saucepan. Add the boiling water and salt. Stir well, bring to the boil and cook gently for 10 minutes. Leave to cool, then tip into a bowl.

2 Add the peas, raisins, celery, spring onions and chilli. Mix the oil, white wine vinegar, lime zest and juice and add to the salad. Season to taste with salt and pepper.

3 Gently fold the smoked chicken into the bulghar and leave to stand for at least 1 hour to allow the flavours to develop.

4 Reserve 6 black olives for garnishing, then chop all the rest. Mix with the remaining ingredients for the dressing and season with black pepper.

5 Pile the bulghar and chicken mixture on to large plates. Put a black olive in the centre of each. Stir the dressing, spoon it around the edge of each plate and serve.

Warm duck breast salad
with courgettes and fresh raspberries

*Pan-fried duck breasts, sliced and arranged on a bed of tender young salad leaves,
red onions and diced, blanched courgettes, served with a warm fresh raspberry
dressing and garnished with shreds of crispy duck skin.*

SERVES 6

6 duck breasts

5 ml/1 tsp celery salt

**3 small courgettes (zucchini), quartered
lengthways and cut into small chunks**

2 heads of chicory (Belgian endive)

100 g/4 oz lamb's tongue lettuce

50 g/2 oz wild rocket

**1 head of radicchio, separated
into leaves**

**2 small red onions, sliced and
separated into rings**

120 ml/4 fl oz/½ cup olive oil

60 ml/4 tbsp raspberry vinegar

60 ml/4 tbsp balsamic vinegar

30 ml/2 tbsp red wine vinegar

5 ml/1 tsp Dijon mustard

5 ml/1 tsp caster (superfine) sugar

Salt and freshly ground black pepper

100 g/4 oz fresh raspberries

**45 ml/3 tbsp finely chopped fresh
parsley, for garnishing**

1 Using a sharp pointed knife, remove the sinew that runs from the pointed end of the underside of the duck breasts. This stops them curling up when cooked. Season the duck skin with the celery salt.

2 Heat a large frying pan (skillet), add the breasts, skin-sides down, and fry (sauté) over a moderate heat for about 4 minutes until the fat runs and the skin is golden brown. Turn the breasts over and cook for a further 4–6 minutes until cooked to your liking.

3 Remove from the pan, carefully take the skin off, then wrap the breasts in foil and keep warm. Return the skin to the frying pan. Turn up the heat and cook until crisp, then remove and drain on kitchen paper (paper towels). Cut into shreds and reserve for garnishing.

4 Blanch the courgettes in boiling water for 2 minutes. Drain, rinse with cold water and drain again.

5 Cut a cone shape out of the base of each head of chicory, then separate into leaves and cut into pieces. Mix with the lamb's tongue lettuce, the rocket and radicchio leaves (tearing up any large pieces of radicchio). Add the courgettes and onion rings. Pile on very large plates.

6 Cut the duck breasts diagonally into slices and arrange on top of the salads.

7 Spoon all but 45 ml/3 tbsp of the duck fat from the pan. Add the oil, vinegars, mustard, sugar and some salt and pepper to the pan juices and bring to the boil, stirring. Add the raspberries, then spoon the mixture over the duck and salads, letting the dressing trickle round the plate edges.

8 Put a few shreds of duck skin on top of the duck, scatter a little finely chopped parsley around and serve.

Café style Rocket, or *arugula*, to give it its Italian name, has a delicious pungent, peppery taste and aroma that are perfect in salads. It comes in two forms – wild rocket, which has a jagged leaf, similar to dandelion, and cultivated rocket, which has a smoother appearance. Raw rocket is often piled on top of a pizza, but you can serve it wilted, like spinach. Try it chopped and mashed into butter with a little chopped parsley, to top grilled (broiled) steaks, chops, chicken or fish.

Chicken, avocado and mango salad
in a spiced mayonnaise

*Slices of grilled chicken breast, slivers of avocado and diced fresh mango, folded into
mayonnaise flavoured with cumin and cayenne, served on wild and long-grain rice,
and garnished with toasted pine nuts. See photograph opposite page 96.*

SERVES 6

350 g/12 oz/1½ cups wild rice mix

45 ml/3 tbsp lemon juice

45 ml/3 tbsp sunflower oil, plus a little
extra for brushing

15 ml/1 tbsp sesame oil

Salt and freshly ground black pepper

6 corn-fed chicken breasts

175 ml/6 fl oz/¾ cup mayonnaise

5 ml/1 tsp ground cumin

1.5 ml/¼ tsp cayenne

5 ml/1 tsp clear honey

45 ml/3 tbsp single (light) cream

3 ripe avocados

1 large ripe mango

1 bunch of spring onions (scallions)

50 g/2 oz/½ cup toasted pine nuts

FOR THE GARNISH

6 sprigs of fresh coriander (cilantro)

18 thin slices of cucumber

1 Cook the wild rice mix according to the packet instructions. Drain, rinse with cold water and drain again. Place in a bowl. Whisk 30 ml/ 2 tbsp of the lemon juice with the oils and season to taste. Pour over the rice and toss gently.

2 Brush the chicken breasts with a little sunflower oil. Season lightly, then place on foil on a grill (broiler) rack and grill for 3–4 minutes on each side until golden and cooked through. Leave to cool, then cut diagonally into slices.

3 Mix the mayonnaise with the cumin, cayenne, honey, cream and the remaining lemon juice.

4 Peel, halve, stone (pit) and slice the avocados. Peel the mango, score into dice and cut the flesh off the stone. Trim and chop the spring onions, reserve a little of the green tops for garnishing.

5 Gently fold the chicken, avocado and spring onions into the mayonnaise mixture.

6 Spoon a ring of dressed rice on to each large plate and pile the chicken mixture into the centre. Sprinkle the chicken with the reserved spring onion. Lay a long sprig of coriander at the side of each plate with three slices of cucumber and serve.

Hints and variations A salad-leaf garnish also looks good on this dish.

Café style Wild rice mix, a mixture of long-grain rice and wild rice (which is actually a grass!), can be bought in supermarkets.

MAIN COURSE SALADS

Warm lambs' liver and sweet pear salad
with crispy bacon and baby forcemeat balls

Thin, tender strips of lambs' liver, sautéed in olive oil and unsalted butter, and slices of sweet pear in a dressing of chopped shallots, red wine and wine vinegar, set on a bed of salad leaves and garnished with tiny balls of golden fried herb forcemeat.

SERVES 6

FOR THE FORCEMEAT BALLS
100 g/4 oz/2 cups fresh white breadcrumbs

30 ml/2 tbsp chopped fresh parsley

30 ml/2 tbsp chopped fresh thyme

30 ml/2 tbsp snipped fresh chives

Salt and freshly ground black pepper

1 large egg, beaten

Sunflower oil, for shallow-frying

FOR THE SALAD
12 rashers (slices) of unsmoked streaky bacon, rinded and chopped

25 g/1 oz/2 tbsp unsalted (sweet) butter

120 ml/4 fl oz/½ cup olive oil

6 shallots, finely chopped

700 g/1½ lb lambs' liver, trimmed and cut into thin strips

120 ml/4 fl oz/½ cup red wine

120 ml/4 fl oz/½ cup apple juice

2.5 ml/½ tsp dried herbes de Provence

5 ml/1 tsp caster (superfine) sugar

2 eating (dessert) pears

10 ml/2 tsp lemon juice

250 g/9 oz mixed salad leaves

100 g/4 oz radishes, sliced

60 ml/4 tbsp red wine vinegar

6 sprigs of fresh flatleaf parsley, for garnishing

1 Put the breadcrumbs in a bowl and stir in the parsley, thyme and chives. Season well with salt and pepper, then mix with the beaten egg to bind. Shape the mixture into 30 very small balls.

2 Heat the oil for shallow-frying in a large frying pan (skillet) and fry (sauté) the balls, turning once or twice, for about 3 minutes until golden. Drain on kitchen paper (paper towels) and keep warm. Drain off the oil, then wipe out the pan with kitchen paper.

3 Dry-fry the bacon until crisp and remove from the pan with a draining spoon. Reserve. Add the butter and 60 ml/4 tbsp of the olive oil to the bacon fat. Fry the shallots for 2 minutes, stirring. Add the liver and fry, stirring, for a further minute.

4 Add the red wine, apple juice, dried herbs, sugar and a little salt and pepper and cook quickly for 3 minutes until nearly all the liquid has evaporated, stirring all the time.

5 Quarter and core the pears and cut into thin slices. Mix with the lemon juice to prevent browning.

6 Mix the salad leaves with the radishes and pile on six large plates. Arrange the pear slices to one side. Spoon the liver mixture over the salad.

7 Quickly add the remaining oil and the vinegar to the pan and bring to the boil, stirring. Season to taste. Spoon the dressing over the salad and top with the warm crispy forcemeat balls and the bacon. Lay a thin sprig of flatleaf parsley to one side on each plate and serve.

Beef fillet and baby vegetable salad
with mustard and honey dressing

Prime beef fillet, marinated in red wine and juniper berries, quickly roasted, cut into slivers, drizzled with a grain-mustard and honey dressing, and served with a warm baby vegetable salad.

SERVES 6

700 g/1½ lb piece of beef fillet

150 ml/¼ pt/⅔ cup red wine

30 ml/2 tbsp olive oil

12 juniper berries, roughly crushed

Salt and freshly ground black pepper

1 bay leaf

FOR THE SALAD

450 g/1 lb baby new potatoes, scrubbed

225 g/8 oz baby carrots, scrubbed

100 g/4 oz mangetout (snow peas)

100 g/4 oz baby corn cobs, cut into short lengths

30 ml/2 tbsp extra-virgin olive oil

15 ml/1 tbsp lemon juice

50 g/2 oz lamb's tongue lettuce

1 bunch of spring onions (scallions), trimmed and cut into short lengths

1 Put the meat in a shallow dish. Whisk the wine with the olive oil, the juniper berries, a pinch of salt and a good grinding of pepper. Pour over the meat, turn to coat and add the bay leaf, broken into two or three pieces. Leave to marinate for 6 hours or overnight, if possible, turning occasionally.

2 Preheat the oven to 220°C/425°F/gas 7/fan oven 200°C.

3 Remove the meat from the marinade and place in a roasting tin (pan). Roast in the preheated oven for 30 minutes for rare, 45 minutes for well done. Remove from the oven, leave until completely cold, then wrap in clingfilm (plastic wrap) and chill.

4 Put the potatoes and carrots together in a pan of boiling, lightly salted water. Put the mangetout and corn cobs in a steamer or metal colander over the pan, cover and steam for about 4 minutes until cooked but still with some 'bite'. Remove the steamer. Continue to cook the potatoes and carrots until just tender. Drain.

5 Put all the vegetables in a large mixing bowl. Spoon the extra-virgin olive oil over and add the lemon juice and a little salt and pepper. Toss gently, leave to cool, then stir in the lettuce and spring onions and chill.

FOR THE DRESSING

60 ml/4 tbsp extra-virgin olive oil

30 ml/2 tbsp grainy mustard

30 ml/2 tbsp red wine vinegar

15 ml/1 tbsp lemon juice

30 ml/2 tbsp clear honey

15 ml/1 tbsp chopped fresh parsley

TO FINISH

90 ml/6 tbsp mayonnaise

45 ml/3 tbsp crème fraîche

6 Whisk together all the dressing ingredients, seasoning to taste with salt and pepper. Mix the mayonnaise and crème fraîche together in a separate bowl.

7 With a very sharp knife, carve the beef into thin slivers. Pile the vegetables on six plates. Loosely curl up the slices of beef and arrange attractively to one side. Drizzle the dressing over the meat, put a spoonful of the mayonnaise cream to one side and serve.

Hints and variations You must use a very sharp knife to cut the beef as the slices should be very thin. When you arrange them on the plates, aim for a constructed but carelessly crumpled heap – you don't want them to look too formal!

Café style The juniper berries in this recipe add an unusual spicy, aromatic flavour. They are perhaps best known as the predominant flavour in gin, but they may be used, crushed, to flavour beef, pork and pâtés. They are also good in stuffings and even in fruit cake.

MAIN COURSE SALADS

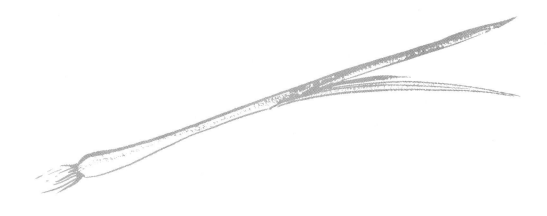

Chargrilled sardine salad
with horseradish dressing

Fresh sardines, stuffed with aromatic sprigs of thyme and flame-grilled, with baby new potatoes, sliced Mediterranean tomatoes, red onions and hard-boiled eggs on a bed of shredded cos lettuce, all drizzled with a creamy horseradish dressing.

SERVES 6

700 g/1½ lb new potatoes

1 large sprig of fresh mint

6 eggs

12 large or 18 small sardines, cleaned

Salt and freshly ground black pepper

1 bunch of fresh thyme

30 ml/2 tbsp olive oil

6 beefsteak tomatoes, sliced

3 red onions, sliced

2 heads of cos (romaine) lettuce

45 ml/3 tbsp lemon juice

30 ml/2 tbsp extra-virgin olive oil

FOR THE DRESSING

150 ml/¼ pt/⅔ cup crème fraîche

45 ml/3 tbsp sunflower oil

30 ml/2 tbsp lemon juice

60 ml/4 tbsp creamed horseradish

200 ml/7 fl oz/scant 1 cup milk

FOR THE GARNISH
Wedges of lemon

Sprigs of fresh thyme and parsley

1 Scrape the potatoes and cut into bite-sized pieces. Scrub the eggs under cold running water.

2 Put the potato pieces and eggs in boiling lightly salted water with the sprig of mint and cook for 10 minutes. Put the eggs in cold water. Test the potatoes and cook a little longer, if necessary. Drain the potatoes, rinse with cold water and drain again.

3 Scrape the scales off the sardines. Rinse the fish under cold running water. Pat dry inside and out with kitchen paper (paper towels). Season the insides with salt and pepper, then push some thyme into each one.

4 Brush with olive oil and lay on foil on a grill (broiler) rack. Set aside until ready to cook. Shell and quarter the eggs.

5 Arrange the tomatoes towards the edges of large plates. Separate the onions into rings and scatter over. Arrange the hard-boiled eggs attractively on the top. Mix the potatoes and lettuce together, toss in the lemon juice and the olive oil and pile in the centre.

6 Make the dressing. Whisk all the ingredients together with a little salt and pepper until smooth, thinning, if necessary, with a little more milk to form a thick, pouring dressing.

7 Grill (broil) the sardines under a preheated grill for 3–4 minutes on each side until charred on the outside and meltingly soft in the centre. You may need to cook the fish in two batches, keeping the first lot warm while you cook the remainder.

8 Transfer the fish to plates of salad. Drizzle the dressing around and garnish with wedges of lemon and sprigs of fresh thyme and parsley before serving.

Salmon, new potato and pink grapefruit salad
with lemon mayonnaise

Fresh wild salmon tails and unsmoked lardons, pan-fried, then piled on a salad of warm new potatoes, cherry tomatoes, mixed salad leaves and pink grapefruit segments and finished with a warm lemon dressing.

SERVES 6

3 pink grapefruit

700 g/1½ lb baby new potatoes, scraped and cut into bite-sized pieces

150 ml/¼ pt/⅔ cup extra-virgin olive oil

100 g/4 oz unsmoked lardons

225 g/8 oz mixed salad leaves

1 red onion, thinly sliced and separated into rings

100 g/4 oz cherry tomatoes, halved

6 wild salmon tail fillets, about 175 g/6 oz each

300 ml/½ pt/1¼ cups mayonnaise

Finely grated zest and juice of 1 lemon

60 ml/4 tbsp red wine vinegar

15 ml/1 tbsp light brown sugar

Salt and freshly ground black pepper

1 Holding the fruit over a bowl to catch the juice, cut all the peel and pith off the grapefruit with a serrated knife and discard. Separate the fruit into segments and put them to one side. Squeeze the membranes over the bowl to extract any remaining juice.

2 Boil the potatoes in lightly salted water for about 10 minutes or until tender. Drain.

3 Meanwhile, heat 30 ml/2 tbsp of the oil in a frying pan (skillet). Fry (sauté) the lardons until golden and cooked. Remove with a draining spoon and drain on kitchen paper (paper towels).

4 Mix the salad leaves with the potatoes and bacon and pile on six large plates. Scatter the grapefruit segments, onion rings and tomatoes over.

5 Reheat the frying pan and fry the salmon fillets, skin-sides up, for 2–3 minutes. Turn over and cook for a further 3 minutes until the salmon is cooked. Carefully lay a fillet on each salad.

6 Mix the mayonnaise with the lemon zest and 5 ml/1 tsp of the juice.

7 Quickly add the remaining olive oil, the vinegar, grapefruit juice and sugar to the pan. Bring to the boil, stirring. Season to taste and add a dash more vinegar, if liked.

8 Spoon the dressing over the salads and fish. Put a spoonful of the lemon mayonnaise to the side of each and serve.

MAIN COURSE SALADS

Salade Niçoise
with new potatoes, beans and quails' eggs

*Baby waxy new potatoes, thin French beans, hard-boiled quails' eggs, juicy young
peas and rich salted anchovies, tossed with cherry tomatoes, olives and caper berries
in a herb-flavoured oil and vinegar dressing, then piled into lettuce-lined bowls.*

SERVES 6

**700 g/1½ lb waxy new potatoes,
scrubbed and cut into bite-sized pieces**

**350 g/12 oz very fine French (green)
beans, topped, tailed and halved**

12 quails' eggs

100 g/4 oz jar of salted anchovy fillets

100 g/4 oz black olives

75 g/3 oz caperberries

18 cherry tomatoes, halved

**100 g/4 oz shelled fresh or
cooked frozen peas**

**1 small onion, thinly sliced and
separated into rings**

90 ml/6 tbsp olive oil

30 ml/2 tbsp red wine vinegar

Salt and freshly ground black pepper

30 ml/2 tbsp chopped fresh tarragon

30 ml/2 tbsp chopped fresh parsley

30 ml/2 tbsp snipped fresh chives

**1 large round lettuce,
separated into leaves**

1 Boil the new potatoes in lightly salted water in a large saucepan for about 10 minutes. At the end of this time, put the beans in a steamer over the saucepan and steam for about 6 minutes until just tender but still with some 'bite'. Drain the potatoes, rinse with cold water and drain again. Return to the saucepan.

2 Boil the quails' eggs for 3 minutes. Plunge into cold water, then shell and cut in half.

3 Soak the anchovies in cold water for 10 minutes. Drain and pat dry on kitchen paper (paper towels).

4 Add the fish to the potatoes with the beans, olives, caperberries, tomatoes, peas and onion rings. Drizzle the oil and vinegar over and add a sprinkling of salt, a good grinding of pepper and all the herbs. Toss gently.

5 Line six large bowls with lettuce leaves, then spoon the mixture into the centre. Arrange the egg halves on top and serve.

Café style Capers and caperberries are both useful for flavouring dishes, but don't get them confused! Capers, which are the immature flower buds of a Mediterranean shrub, are quite small, whereas caperberries, which are the fruit of the plant, are much larger and are harvested with their stalks. Both are sold pickled and, once opened, should be stored in the fridge. Capers are used for flavouring sauces, particularly for fish dishes. Caperberries are delicious as a cocktail nibble or in salads.

desserts and cheese

For many people, the sweets are the best part of the meal.
Café-style desserts usually reflect the best of each of the
main influences – ice creams from Italy, pastries and pancakes
from France, creams and mousses from all over the
Mediterranean and, often, the occasional English nursery
pudding given a specially stylish treatment. All these are
reflected in the creations in this chapter and, for those
with a less sweet tooth, there are some cheese dishes.
As with the other courses, presentation as well as
innovation are the keynotes.
Remember not to make the portions too big, as your guests
will already be fairly full, and many desserts are quite rich.

Gelato espresso
with amaretti biscuits

Soft ice cream made with brandy and chocolate chips and served with an amaretti biscuit, presented with a tiny glass of scalding hot espresso on the side to pour over just before eating.

DESSERTS AND CHEESE

SERVES 6

3 eggs, separated

75 g/3 oz/¹⁄₃ cup caster (superfine) sugar

100 g/4 oz/1 cup chocolate chips

250 ml/8 fl oz/1 cup double (heavy) cream

45 ml/3 tbsp brandy

75 g/3 oz/³⁄₄ cup plain (semi-sweet) chocolate

6 individually wrapped amaretti biscuits (cookies)

300 ml/¹⁄₂ pt/1¹⁄₄ cups hot espresso coffee

1 Whisk the egg yolks and sugar until thick and pale. Fold in the chocolate chips.

2 Whip the cream with the brandy until peaking and fold in with a metal spoon.

3 Turn the mixture into a freezer-proof container and freeze until firm. Remove from the freezer 10 minutes before serving to soften slightly.

4 Meanwhile, make the chocolate caraque for the decoration. Melt the chocolate in a bowl over a pan of simmering water or heat briefly in the microwave. Spread thinly on a marble slab or other cold surface and leave until just set. Holding the edge of a long knife blade almost upright on the chocolate, shave off long curls of chocolate with a slight sawing movement, side to side. Chill until ready to use.

5 When ready to serve, scoop the ice cream into small glass bowls. Decorate each with the chocolate curls. Put the dishes on plates. Pour the coffee into shot glasses (put a teaspoon in the glass first to prevent cracking, then remove it).

6 Put each glass beside a dish of ice cream and add an amaretti biscuit. Serve immediately.

Hints and variations If you don't want to make your own ice cream, buy a top-quality rich chocolate or ginger ice cream and serve it in the same way.

Crêpes noisettes
with raspberries and cream

Wafer-thin pancakes filled with sweetened whipped cream and finely chopped hazelnuts, served with a hot fresh raspberry coulis drizzled enticingly over the top and decorated with sprigs of mint.

SERVES 6

250 ml/8 fl oz/1 cup double (heavy) cream

150 ml/¼ pt/⅔ cup thick plain yoghurt

75 g/3 oz/½ cup icing (confectioners') sugar, plus extra for dusting

100 g/4 oz/1 cup hazelnuts (filberts), finely chopped

2.5 ml/½ tsp vanilla essence (extract)

350 g/12 oz fresh raspberries

5 ml/1 tsp lemon juice

FOR THE PANCAKES
175 g/6 oz/1½ cups plain (all-purpose) flour

A pinch of salt

2 eggs

450 ml/¾ pt/2 cups milk

20 g/¾ oz/1½ tbsp butter, melted

Sunflower oil, for cooking

FOR THE DECORATION
50 g/2 oz/½ cup toasted hazelnuts

6 small sprigs of fresh mint

1 Make the filling. Whip the cream and yoghurt with 50 g/2 oz/⅓ cup of the icing sugar. Fold in the nuts and vanilla essence. Chill until ready to use.

2 Reserve 100 g/4 oz of the raspberries and put the remainder in a pan with the remaining icing sugar. Heat gently until the juice runs, stirring occasionally. Purée in a blender or food processor, then rub the mixture through a fine sieve (strainer) to remove the seeds. Return to the saucepan and stir in the lemon juice.

3 Make the pancakes. Sift the flour and salt into a bowl. Make a well in the centre and add the eggs and half the milk. Beat well until smooth. Stir in the remaining milk and the melted butter. Leave to stand, if possible, for 30 minutes.

4 Heat a little oil in an omelette pan and pour off the excess. When very hot, pour in a just enough batter to coat the base of the pan when tipped around. Cook until the top is set and the base is golden. Flip over with a palette knife or toss and cook the other side until golden. Slide out on to a plate, cover and keep warm over a pan of gently simmering water. Repeat until all the batter is used. It should make 24 small, thin pancakes.

5 When ready to serve, reheat the raspberry coulis. Fold the pancakes into quarters. Open up gently and add a spoonful of hazelnut cream to each.

6 Arrange four overlapping on each plate. Drizzle with a little raspberry coulis and scatter a few nuts and raspberries over. Decorate each with a sprig of mint and serve.

Café style Serve these on plain white plates, if you can – the contrast with the rich red of the coulis is fabulous.

Crème brûlée
with mango and passion fruit

*Diced fresh mango blended with the fragrant, juicy seeds of passion fruit,
topped with yoghurt blended with fresh cream, chilled and glazed with
caramelised sugar. See photograph opposite page 97.*

SERVES 6

2 mangoes

3 passion fruit

450 ml/³/₄ pt/2 cups thick vanilla yoghurt

300 ml/¹/₂ pt/1¹/₄ cups extra-thick cream

**75 g/3 oz/¹/₃ cup caster
(superfine) sugar**

6 rosebuds or freesias, for decoration

1 Peel the mangoes and cut all the flesh off the stones (pits). Dice and place in six ramekin dishes (custard cups).

2 Halve all the passion fruit and scoop out the seeds and pulp from one half into each dish. Mix gently.

3 Mix the yoghurt and cream together and spoon over the fruit.

4 Sprinkle liberally with the sugar. Either use a blow-torch to caramelise the sugar or place the dishes under a preheated grill (broiler) until the sugar turns a rich golden brown. Chill.

5 When ready to serve, place each ramekin on a large plate, and set a rosebud or freesia beside it for decoration.

Hints and variations Use other combinations of fresh soft fruits for this dish. Fresh raspberries and strawberries, melon and stem ginger, and blueberries and red cherries all make particularly good combinations.

An alternative way to caramelise the sugar is to put it in a saucepan and heat gently until it melts. Turn up the heat and boil rapidly until the sugar caramelises (take care not to let it burn). Pour the caramel over the top of the yoghurt and leave until cold before chilling. This gives a smooth glossy top rather than the tortoiseshell effect of caramelising the sugar on the cream.

DESSERTS AND CHEESE

Panna cotta
with crushed strawberries and oranges

A traditional set Italian cream with a hint of vanilla and lemon zest, complemented by the freshness of crushed strawberries and juicy oranges and decorated with thinly pared orange zest.

SERVES 6

45 ml/3 tbsp cold water

1 sachet of powdered gelatine

900 ml/1½ pts/3¾ cups double (heavy) cream

50 g/2 oz/¼ cup caster (superfine) sugar

1 vanilla pod, split

Thinly pared zest of 1 lemon

2 oranges

350 g/12 oz strawberries, hulled

45 ml/3 tbsp strawberry jam (conserve)

1 Put the water in a small bowl and sprinkle the gelatine over. Leave to soften for 5 minutes.

2 Meanwhile, put half the cream in a saucepan with the sugar, vanilla pod and lemon zest. Bring slowly to the boil. Stir in the softened gelatine and stir until completely dissolved. Leave to cool, then remove the vanilla pod and lemon zest.

3 Whip the remaining cream until softly peaking. Fold into the cold, but not set, cream with a metal spoon. Spoon the mixture into six lightly oiled ramekin dishes (custard cups) and chill until set.

4 Meanwhile, thinly pare the zest from the oranges. Cut into thin strips and boil in water for 2 minutes. Drain, rinse with cold water and drain again.

5 Cut all the skin and pith off the oranges. Cut the fruit into slices, then cut each slice into quarters.

6 Crush the strawberries in a bowl with a fork. Stir in the jam and stir until dissolved. Add the orange pieces and crush lightly.

7 When ready to serve, turn the creams out on to plates. Spoon the crushed fruits around. Top the creams with the shreds of orange zest and serve.

Café style The rich red and orange of the fruits look wonderful set on white plates. Alternatively, a contrasting plain colour, such as blue, green or black will set them off perfectly.

French apple tart
with blackcurrant crème

A sweet, melting pastry case filled with caramel-glazed dessert apples nestling on a velvety frangipane, served with gently poached blackcurrants folded through cool crème fraîche.

SERVES 6

FOR THE PASTRY (PASTE)

225 g/8 oz/2 cups plain (all-purpose) flour

A pinch of salt

200 g/7 oz/scant 1 cup butter, diced

25 g/1 oz/2 tbsp caster (superfine) sugar

1 egg yolk

FOR THE FILLING

½ vanilla pod, split

300 ml/½ pt/1¼ cups milk

15 g/½ oz/2 tbsp cornflour (cornstarch)

15 g/½ oz/2 tbsp plain (all-purpose) flour

50 g/2 oz/¼ cup caster sugar

1 large egg, beaten

3 Golden Delicious eating (dessert) apples

15 ml/1 tbsp lemon juice

25 g/1 oz/3 tbsp icing (confectioners') sugar, plus extra for dusting

1 Make the pastry. Sift the flour and the salt into a bowl. Add the butter and rub in with your fingertips. Stir in the caster sugar. Add the egg yolk and work with a knife, then your hands, until the mixture forms a firm ball. Wrap in clingfilm (plastic wrap) and chill for 30 minutes.

2 Preheat the oven to 200°C/400°F/gas 6/fan oven 180°C. Grease a 23 cm/9 in loose-bottomed fluted flan tin (pie pan).

3 Roll out the pastry and use to line the prepared tin. Prick the base with a fork. Fill with crumpled foil and bake in the preheated oven for 10 minutes. Remove the foil and return to the oven for 5 minutes to dry out.

4 Meanwhile, make the filliing. Put the vanilla pod and milk in a saucepan. Bring to the boil, then remove from the heat and leave to infuse for 10 minutes, then discard the pod.

5 Blend the cornflour with the flour and the sugar in a saucepan with a little of the milk. Whisk the egg into the remaining milk, then strain into the flour mixture. Bring to the boil and cook for 2 minutes, stirring all the time, until thick and smooth.

6 Spoon this mixture into the cooked pastry case (pie shell).

7 Quarter, core and thinly slice the apples and toss in the lemon juice. Arrange attractively in the pie shell, covering the frangipane. Scatter liberally with the icing sugar and bake in the oven for 20 minutes until the sugar has caramelised. Remove from the oven.

FOR THE BLACKCURRANT CRÈME

175 g/6 oz fresh or thawed frozen
blackcurrants

25 g/1 oz/2 tbsp caster sugar

15 ml/1 tbsp cornflour

15 ml/1 tbsp water

300 ml/½ pt/1¼ cups crème fraîche

8 Meanwhile, make the crème. Put the blackcurrants in a saucepan with the caster sugar and cornflour. Stir in the water, then heat gently, stirring, for 2–3 minutes until the juice runs and thickens but the fruit is still holding its shape. Remove from the heat and leave to cool.

9 When ready to serve, fold the crème fraîche into the fruit. Cut the warm tart into wedges. Transfer the wedges to plates with a spoonful of blackberry crème to one side. Dust the plates with sifted icing sugar and serve.

Café style Even though this is a dessert, serve it on large plates, so that there is plenty of space to arrange everything attractively.

Lemon tart
with Grand Marnier sabayon

A classic, refreshing lemon tart in a crisp, buttery pastry, complemented by the warm, sweet subtleties of a foamy egg-custard sauce laced with a sophisticated dash of Grand Marnier.

SERVES 6

FOR THE PASTRY (PASTE)
175 g/6 oz/1½ cups plain (all-purpose) flour

50 g/2 oz/½ cup self-raising (self-rising) flour

A pinch of salt

40 g/1½ oz/¼ cup icing (confectioners') sugar

100 g/4 oz/½ cup butter, diced

About 45 ml/3 tbsp cold water, to mix

FOR THE FILLING
2 lemons

75 g/3 oz/⅓ cup butter

5 eggs

90 g/3½ oz/scant½ cup caster (superfine) sugar

FOR THE SAUCE
2 eggs

25 g/1 oz/2 tbsp caster sugar

150 ml/¼ pt/⅔ cup Grand Marnier

1 Preheat the oven to 200°C/400°F/gas 6/fan oven 180°C.

2 Make the pastry. Sift the flours, salt and half the icing sugar into a bowl. Add the butter and rub in with your fingertips. Mix with enough cold water to form a firm dough.

3 Knead gently on a lightly floured surface. Roll out and use to line a 23 cm/9 in loose-bottomed flan tin (pie pan). Prick the base with a fork and fill with crumpled foil.

4 Bake in the preheated oven for 10 minutes. Remove the foil and bake for a further 5 minutes to dry out. Remove from the oven. Turn down the heat to 140°C/275°F/gas 1/fan oven 125°C.

5 Thinly pare the zest of one of the lemons, cut into very thin shreds and boil in water for 1 minute. Drain, rinse with cold water and drain again.

6 To make the filling, finely grate the zest from the other lemon and squeeze the juice from both.

7 Melt the butter. Whisk in the grated lemon zest and the juice, the eggs and the caster sugar. When thoroughly blended, pour into the flan case (pie shell).

8 Cook the tart in the cool oven for 30 minutes until lightly set. Remove from the oven, leave to cool, then chill.

9 When almost ready to serve, make the sauce. Put the eggs with the sugar and Grand Marnier in a bowl over a pan of simmering water. Whisk with an electric or hand whisk until thick and foamy. To serve, dust the tart with the remaining icing sugar and cut into six portions. Put a tiny cluster of lemon zest on the edge of each slice of tart. Spoon a pool of sauce on to each of six plates, place a piece of tart in the centre of each pool and serve.

Fresh fruit medley on honey almond jelly
with almond tuiles

A light and refreshing dessert of a selection of exotic fruits, beautifully arranged and set in a milky-white almond-flavoured jelly and served with golden almond tuile biscuits.

SERVES 6

FOR THE TUILES

75 g/3 oz/⅓ cup unsalted (sweet) butter

75 g/3 oz/⅓ cup caster (superfine) sugar

50 g/2 oz/½ cup plain (all-purpose) flour

75 g/3 oz/¾ cup flaked (slivered) almonds

FOR THE JELLY

600 ml/1 pt/2½ cups milk

15 ml/1 tbsp/1 sachet of powdered gelatine

30 ml/2 tbsp clear honey

2.5 ml/½ tsp natural almond essence (extract)

1 papaya (pawpaw)

2 kiwi fruit

2 star fruit

1 pomegranate

1 Preheat the oven to 200°C/400°F/gas 6/fan oven 180°C.

2 Beat the butter and sugar together until light and fluffy.

3 Work in the flour and almonds.

4 Put 5 ml/1 tsp mounds of the mixture on a baking (cookie) sheet, lined with non-stick baking parchment. Flatten with a wet palette knife.

5 Bake in the preheated oven for about 7 minutes until lightly golden. Lift off the sheet and quickly curl round a rolling pin until firm. Cool on a wire rack.

6 Make the jelly. Pour 90 ml/6 tbsp of the milk into a small bowl. Add the gelatine and leave to soften for 5 minutes. Stand the bowl in a pan of hot water or heat briefly in the microwave until completely dissolved. Do not allow to boil.

7 Stir this mixture into the remaining milk with the honey and almond essence. Pour into six large, shallow dishes (flat soup plates are ideal). Leave in a cool place until just set.

8 Meanwhile, peel the papaya, halve, scoop out the seeds and slice the fruit. Peel and slice the kiwi fruit. Slice the star fruit across the fruit, to give star-shaped pieces.

9 Arrange the prepared fruits attractively on the jelly. Scoop out the pomegranate seeds and dot a few in between the fruit slices. Put two almond tuiles to one side of each plate, or hand them separately.

Hints and variations The tuile mixture makes 18 biscuits (cookies), which is more than you need, but it allows for breakages and nibbling!

Rhubarb and ginger mousse
with chilled crème anglaise

A sensational marriage of rhubarb and ginger, folded through a snow of meringue and whipped cream and allowed to set lightly, then served surrounded by a smooth custard sauce.

SERVES 6

FOR THE MOUSSE
450 g/1 lb champagne rhubarb, cut into chunks

90 ml/6 tbsp water

175 g/6 oz/³⁄₄ cup caster (superfine) sugar

15 ml/1 tbsp/1 sachet of powdered gelatine

2 pieces of stem ginger in syrup

3 egg whites

300 ml/½ pt/1¼ cups double (heavy) cream

FOR THE CUSTARD
300 ml/½ pt/1¼ cups milk

3 egg yolks

1 vanilla pod, split

45 ml/3 tbsp ginger syrup from the jar of stem ginger

45 ml/3 tbsp single (light) cream

12 physalis

1 Put the rhubarb in a pan with the water and 25 g/1 oz/2 tbsp of the sugar. Cover and cook gently for about 10 minutes until pulpy. Tilt the pan and stir in the gelatine, then continue to stir until completely dissolved.

2 Drain the pieces of ginger, chop and put into a blender or food processor with the rhubarb mixture and run the machine until smooth. Tip into a bowl and leave until cold but not set.

3 Whisk the egg whites until stiff. Whisk in half the remaining sugar and whisk again until stiff. Add the rest of the sugar and whisk again.

4 Whip the double cream until peaking. Fold the cream, then the meringue, into the rhubarb and ginger purée. Turn into a dish and chill until set.

5 Meanwhile, put the milk and vanilla pod in a saucepan. Bring slowly to the boil, remove from the heat, cover and leave to infuse for 10 minutes. Remove the pod.

6 Whisk the eggs yolks and the remaining sugar together, then whisk in the flavoured milk. Strain into a clean bowl and place it over a pan of simmering water. Cook, stirring all the time, until the mixture has thickened and will coat the back of a spoon. Do not allow to boil or the mixture will curdle. Remove the bowl from the saucepan. Cover with a circle of wet greaseproof (waxed) paper and leave to cool, then chill.

7 When ready to serve, spoon a pool of the custard on each of six plates. Put a large spoonful of mousse in the centre, so you can see the lovely texture of the mousse. Trickle a spoonful of ginger syrup in a ring around the mousse towards the edge of the custard. Repeat with the cream. Using a cocktail stick (toothpick), draw lines from the centre to the outside of the rings at an angle all the way round, to form a feathered effect.

8 Decorate each plate with two physalis with their papery petals drawn back, revealing the fruit inside, and serve.

Café style Physalis – or Chinese lanterns, as they are also known – are a great way to add an exotic touch to a dessert. They taste delicious, too, having a firm texture and sharp, fruity flavour.

Elderflower and rosemary sorbet
in a brandy snap basket

A delicate sorbet, scented with sweet elderflower and aromatic rosemary and sharpened slightly with the zest of lemon, nestling in a crisp brandy snap basket and decorated with flowers or berries.

SERVES 6

225 g/8 oz/1 cup granulated sugar

175 ml/6 fl oz/³⁄₄ cup elderflower cordial

750 ml/1¼ pts/3 cups water

Thinly pared zest and juice of 2 lemons

2 large sprigs of fresh rosemary

1 large egg white

FOR THE BASKETS

40 g/1½ oz/3 tbsp butter

40 g/1½ oz/3 tbsp caster (superfine) sugar

20 ml/1½ tbsp golden (light corn) syrup

40 g/1½ oz/¹⁄₃ cup plain (all-purpose) flour

2.5 ml/½ tsp ground ginger

5 ml/1 tsp brandy

A small orange, for shaping

TO FINISH

Fresh elderflowers, sprigs of fresh rosemary or bunches of elderberries

Icing (confectioners') sugar and ground ginger, for dusting

1 Put the sugar, cordial and water in a saucepan, heat gently until the sugar dissolves, then boil rapidly for 2 minutes. Remove from the heat, stir in the lemon zest and juice, add the rosemary and cover. Leave to infuse until cold.

2 Whisk the egg white until stiff. Strain the elderflower mixture into the egg white and mix well. Pour the mixture into a freezer-proof container. Freeze for 2 hours or until half-frozen. Whisk thoroughly with a fork to break up the ice crystals. Return to the freezer and freeze until firm.

3 Meanwhile, make the brandy snap baskets. Preheat the oven to 180°C/350°F/gas 4/fan oven 160°C.

4 Melt the butter, caster sugar and syrup in a saucepan over a gentle heat. Stir in the flour, ginger and brandy.

5 Line a baking (cookie) sheet with non-stick baking parchment. Using half the mixture, spoon three mounds of the mixture well apart on the baking sheet. Bake in the preheated oven for about 7 minutes or until golden, well spread out and full of bubbly holes.

6 Grease the small orange. Lift one brandy snap off the baking sheet with a fish slice and quickly mould round the orange. Remove and mould the others in the same way. If they harden before moulding, pop them back in the oven briefly to soften. Cook and mould the remaining three baskets. When cold, store in an airtight container.

7 When ready to serve, put a basket on each of six plates. Fill with scoops of the sorbet. Lay a head of elderflowers or a small sprig of rosemary or a tiny bunch of elderberries to one side, dust the plates with sifted icing sugar and a little ground ginger and serve.

Café style Keep the flowery decorations very small – you don't want the presentation to be over-elaborate.

Baby brioche bread and butter puddings
with butterscotch sauce

*Individual brioches, buttered and filled with dried fruit and custard, baked until crisp
and golden on the outside and soft, creamy and fruity in the centre, and served in a
pool of wicked butterscotch sauce.*

SERVES 6

6 individual brioches

100 g/4 oz/½ cup butter, softened

**400 ml/14 fl oz/1¾ cups crème fraîche,
plus extra for serving**

2 large eggs

Finely grated zest and juice of ½ lemon

**50 g/2 oz/¼ cup caster
(superfine) sugar**

**75 g/3 oz/½ cup dried mixed fruit
(fruit cake mix)**

Freshly grated nutmeg

100 g/4 oz/½ cup light brown sugar

45 ml/3 tbsp golden (light corn) syrup

**120 ml/4 fl oz/½ cup double
(heavy) cream**

1 Preheat the oven to 180°C/350°F/gas 4/fan oven 160°C.

2 Cut a slice off the top of each brioche and pull out most the soft
dough in the middle, leaving a shell about 3 mm/⅓ in thick. Gently
spread the lids and the brioches, both inside and out, with two-
thirds of the butter. Stand the brioches in the sections of a tartlet tin
(patty pan).

3 Beat the crème fraîche, eggs, lemon zest and caster sugar with the
fruit and spoon into the brioches. Dust with a little grated nutmeg.

4 Bake in the preheated oven for about 20–25 minutes. Cover loosely
with foil halfway through cooking if over-browning. Add the 'lids' to
the empty sections of the tartlet tin and cook for 5 more minutes
until the brioches and lids are crisp and golden on the outsides and
the filling is set.

5 Meanwhile, melt the remaining butter with the brown sugar and
syrup in a saucepan. When melted, stir in the cream and simmer
gently for 3 minutes. Remove from the heat and stir in the lemon
juice.

6 Transfer the hot brioches to warm plates. Replace the 'lids' at a
jaunty angle. Spoon the butterscotch sauce over and around, and
put a spoonful of crème fraîche to one side, then serve.

Rum chocolate pots
with cinnamon curls

A rich, sensuous, dark chocolate mousse, flavoured with rum and perfectly complemented with delicate buttery cigarettes russes, lightly spiced with an exotic dash of cinnamon.

SERVES 6

FOR THE MOUSSE
4 eggs, separated

100 g/4 oz/½ cup caster (superfine) sugar

250 g/9 oz/generous 1 cup bitter dark chocolate

2.5 ml/½ tsp vanilla essence (extract)

45 ml/3 tbsp dark rum

FOR THE CURLS
1 egg white

50 g/2 oz/¼ cup caster sugar

25 g/1 oz/¼ cup plain (all-purpose) flour

25 g/1 oz/2 tbsp butter, melted

1.5 ml/¼ tsp ground cinnamon

1 First, make the mousse. Whisk the egg yolks and sugar in a bowl over a pan of gently simmering water until thick and pale. Remove from the pan.

2 Break up the chocolate. Place in a small bowl and stand it in the pan of hot water or heat briefly in the microwave.

3 Using a teaspoon, trickle melted chocolate to make eight small motifs on a piece of non-stick baking parchment on a plate and leave to set (I always make two extra in case of breakages). Chill until firm.

4 Stir the vanilla and rum into the remaining chocolate, then fold into the egg yolk mixture.

5 Whisk the egg whites until stiff and fold into the mixture with a metal spoon. Turn into six individual pots and chill to set.

6 Preheat the oven to 200°C/400°F/gas 6/fan oven 180°C.

7 Make the curls. Whisk the egg white and sugar in a bowl until foamy. Whisk in the flour, melted butter and cinnamon.

8 Put six 10 ml/2 tsp portions of the mixture well apart on a baking (cookie) sheet, lined with non-stick baking parchment. Spread each one to make an oval about 7.5 cm/3 in long. Bake in the preheated oven for about 6 minutes until brown round the edges.

9 Lift, one at a time, off the sheet with a fish slice and immediately wrap round the handle of a wooden spoon. When firm, remove and place on a wire rack. Repeat with the remaining mixture to make 12 curls in all.

TO FINISH

90 ml/6 tbsp crème fraîche

30 ml/2 tbsp icing (confectioners') sugar

30 ml/2 tbsp cocoa (unsweetened chocolate) powder

10 When ready to serve, put a spoonful of crème fraîche on top of each chocolate pot. Carefully slide the motifs off the parchment with a palette knife and stand one in each spoonful of cream.

11 Transfer the pots to plates. Dust the edges of the plates with a mixture of icing sugar and cocoa powder, lay two cinnamon curls to the side of each pot and serve.

Hints and variations You can flavour the chocolate mousse with brandy or orange liqueur instead of rum, if you like. If you are in a hurry, use bought *cigarettes russes* or praline curls instead making your own.

Café style I always use continental dark chocolate for cooking. It has a wonderful, bitter-sweet quality that other chocolates can't match, and its low sugar content allows the full flavour to burst through. Choose one with a cocoa butter content of at least 70 per cent.

127

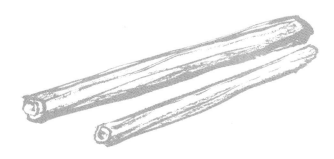

Potted Stilton
with port and frosted grapes

Individual pots of Stilton blended with butter, sweet spices and port, served with a cluster of frosted red and green grapes and slices of thin and crisp, freshly baked melba toast.

SERVES 6

175 g/6 oz ripe Stilton cheese

250 g/9 oz/generous 1 cup butter, softened

1.5 ml/¼ tsp ground mace

1.5 ml/¼ tsp paprika

1.5 ml/¼ tsp made English mustard

45 ml/3 tbsp ruby port

18 juniper berries

6 sage leaves

FOR THE FROSTED GRAPES
1 egg white

6 small bunches of red seedless grapes

6 small bunches of green seedless grapes

60 ml/4 tbsp caster (superfine) sugar

FOR THE TOASTS
6 slices of white or wholemeal bread, crusts removed

1 Cut any rind off the Stilton and discard. Mash the cheese with half the butter, the spices, mustard and port until well blended. Spoon into six very small pots.

2 Melt the remaining butter. Pour a little over the top of each pot, taking care to leave the sediment behind. Press a sage leaf and three juniper berries into the butter, so they are coated. Leave to cool, then chill.

3 Meanwhile, lightly beat the egg white, then brush all over the grapes. Sprinkle with the sugar to coat completely. Leave to dry on non-stick baking parchment.

4 Make the toasts. Preheat the oven to 180°C/350°F/gas 4/fan oven 160°C. Cut each slice of bread into quarters to form four small squares. Roll each one with a rolling pin to flatten.

5 Place on a baking (cookie) sheet and bake in the preheated oven for 10 minutes. Turn the squares over and bake for a further 10 minutes until crisp and golden brown. Cool on a wire rack.

6 Put a pot of Stilton on each of six plates. Lay the frosted grapes and melba toasts to one side and serve.

Amaretti tiramisu
with chocolate fondant

Amaretti biscuits, steeped in Amaretto-flavoured coffee, layered with a fluffy Mascarpone cheese mousse, chilled and served with a creamy milk chocolate fondant sauce.

SERVES 6

90 ml/6 tbsp Amaretto liqueur

90 ml/6 tbsp strong black coffee

225 g/8 oz amaretti biscuits (cookies), roughly crushed

2 large eggs, separated

150 ml/¼ pt/⅔ cup double (heavy) cream

500 g/18 oz/2¼ cups Mascarpone cheese

25 g/1 oz/2 tbsp caster (superfine) sugar

250 ml/8 fl oz/1 cup crème fraîche

FOR THE SAUCE

200 g/7 oz/1¾ cups milk chocolate

25 g/1 oz/2 tbsp butter

60 ml/4 tbsp milk

30 ml/2 tbsp golden (light corn) syrup

30 ml/2 tbsp drinking (sweetened) chocolate powder

18 chocolate coffee beans, for decorating

1 Mix the liqueur and coffee together. Add the biscuit crumbs and leave to soak until they have absorbed the liquid.

2 Whisk the egg whites until stiff.

3 Whip the cream until softly peaking, then whisk in the cheese, sugar and egg yolks. Fold in the egg whites with a metal spoon.

4 Spoon half the biscuit mixture into the base of a shallow, rectangular 1.2 litre/2 pt/5 cup dish. Top with half the cheese mixture. Repeat the layers. Spread the top with the crème fraîche. Chill until firm.

5 Break up the chocolate and place in a saucepan. Add the butter, milk and syrup and heat gently, stirring all the time, until melted and smooth. Remove from the heat but keep slightly warm.

6 When ready to serve, carefully cut the tiramisu into six portions. Transfer each one to a plate, using a fish slice. Trickle a little warm sauce around. Dust the edges of the plates with drinking chocolate powder through a fine sieve (strainer) and scatter three chocolate coffee beans on each plate.

Angel's food cake
with blueberries and pistachios

A light-as-air pistachio gâteau, filled with a layer of crushed blueberry and crème de cassis mousse, smothered in a sweetened fromage frais and whipped cream frosting, and decorated with whole blueberries and pistachio nuts.

SERVES 6

FOR THE CAKE
75 g/3 oz/³⁄₄ cup shelled pistachio nuts

6 egg whites

A pinch of salt

5 ml/1 tsp cream of tartar

225 g/8 oz/1 cup caster (superfine) sugar

65 g/2¹⁄₂ oz/scant ³⁄₄ cup plain (all-purpose) flour

40 g/1¹⁄₂ oz/¹⁄₃ cup cornflour (cornstarch)

5 ml/1 tsp vanilla essence (extract)

FOR THE FILLING AND FROSTING
5 ml/1 tsp powdered gelatine

15 ml/1 tbsp crème de cassis

150 ml/¹⁄₄ pt/²⁄₃ cup double (heavy) cream, plus extra for decorating

25 g/1 oz/3 tbsp icing (confectioners') sugar, plus extra for dusting

150 ml/¹⁄₄ pt/²⁄₃ cup fromage frais

125 g/4¹⁄₂ oz blueberries

1 Preheat the oven to 160°C/325°F/gas 3/fan oven 145°C. Flour the base and sides of a deep, round 18 cm/7 in cake tin (pan) but do not grease.

2 Put the pistachios in a bowl. Cover with boiling water and leave to stand for 5 minutes. Drain, then rub off the skins with a clean disposable kitchen cloth. Reserve half the nuts for decorating and finely chop the remainder.

3 Whisk the egg whites until frothy, then whisk in the salt and cream of tartar and continue to whisk until stiff.

4 Sift the sugar and flours together twice. Lightly fold into the egg whites a little at a time, using a metal spoon. Add the vanilla essence at the same time. Lastly, fold in the chopped nuts.

5 Spoon the mixture into the prepared tin and bake in the preheated oven for 45 minutes or until firm to the touch. Leave to cool in the tin.

6 Turn out on to a plate or board.

7 Sprinkle the gelatine over the cassis in a small bowl. Leave to soften for 5 minutes, then stand the bowl in a pan of gently simmering water and stir until completely dissolved. Do not try to do this in the microwave as the amount is too small.

8 Whip the cream with the icing sugar until peaking, then whisk in the fromage frais. Crush half the blueberries in a bowl with a fork. Stir in the dissolved gelatine. Fold in 75 ml/5 tbsp (about a quarter) of the fromage frais mixture and chill until set.

9   Cut the cake in half horizontally, spread with the blueberry mousse, then sandwich together. Spread the remaining fromage frais frosting all over the cake.

10 To serve, cut the cake into six wedges. Place each one on a plate and dust the plates with a little icing sugar. Decorate the top of each with a few blueberries and pistachios, allowing a couple of each to tumble on to the plate. Trickle a little cream around the edge of the plate and serve.

Hints and variations A flour sifter makes it easy to sift icing sugar round the edge of the plates. An excellent alternative is to use a tea strainer. Work the powder through with a teaspoon, so that it goes exactly where you want it.

Profiteroles
with hot fudge sauce

Golden puffs of light choux pastry, filled to bursting with fresh whipped cream and smothered in a hot, rich fudge sauce made with cream, butter, brown sugar and a hint of vanilla.

SERVES 6

FOR THE PROFITEROLES
150 g/5 oz/1¼ cups plain (all-purpose) flour

A pinch of salt

300 ml/½ pt/1¼ cups water

50 g/2 oz/¼ cup butter

4 eggs, beaten

FOR THE SAUCE
600 ml/1 pt/2½ cups double (heavy) cream, whipped

1 vanilla pod, split

100 g/4 oz/½ cup unsalted (sweet) butter

100 g/4 oz/½ cup light brown sugar

A little icing (confectioners') sugar, for dusting

1 Preheat the oven to 200°C/400°F/gas 6/fan oven 180°C.

2 Sift the flour and salt on to a piece of kitchen paper (paper towel). Put the water and butter in a saucepan and heat until the butter melts, then bring to the boil. Add the flour all in one go and beat with a wooden spoon until the mixture is smooth and leaves the sides of the pan clean.

3 Remove from the heat and gradually beat in the eggs, a little at a time, beating well after each addition until smooth and glossy.

4 Pipe or spoon 42 small balls on to two greased baking (cookie) sheets. Bake one above the other towards the top of the preheated oven for 30 minutes, swapping the positions of the baking sheets after 15 minutes, until puffy and golden brown.

5 Transfer to a wire rack, make a slit in the side of each ball to allow steam to escape and leave to cool.

6 Meanwhile, make the sauce. Put half the cream with all the remaining ingredients in a saucepan. Bring to the boil, reduce the heat and simmer, stirring, for 3 minutes until thick and creamy. Leave to stand until ready to serve.

7 Whip the remaining cream and use to fill the choux balls. Pile seven on each of six small plates.

8 Reheat the sauce, discard the vanilla pod and spoon it over. Dust the edge of the plates with icing sugar and serve.

Hints and variations If you prefer, make 36 slightly larger balls and cook for about 5 minutes longer until crisp and golden.

cocktails and speciality drinks

A colourful cocktail is an exciting and delicious way to start your party. In this chapter, you'll find instructions for making the most popular aperitifs to get your guests' taste buds tingling in anticipation of the meal to come. For anyone driving and those who don't drink alcohol, there are some tempting non-alcoholic options on page 139. Then, to round off the occasion, I have included a wonderful selection of after-dinner drinks, plus some special ways to serve coffee and hot chocolate.

All the recipes make a drink for one person unless stated otherwise.

Daiquiri

Juice of 1 lime

5 ml/1 tsp icing (confectioners') sugar

50 ml/2 fl oz/¼ cup white rum

Cracked ice

1 Mix the lime juice and sugar together in a cocktail glass until dissolved.

2 Stir in the rum and top up the glasses with cracked ice. Serve straight away.

Margarita

Juice of 1 lime

Sea salt

45 ml/3 tbsp tequila

15 ml/1 tbsp orange liqueur

5 ml/1 tsp caster (superfine) sugar

Crushed ice

1 Dip the rim of a cocktail glass in the lime juice, then in sea salt, to give a frosted rim.

2 Whisk the remaining lime juice with the tequila, orange liqueur and sugar, or mix in a cocktail shaker.

3 Fill the cocktail glass with crushed ice and pour the cocktail over. Serve straight away.

Frosted rims As an alternative way to frost the rim of glasses for cocktails, dip the rims in lightly beaten egg white or water, then in caster sugar, and leave to dry. This can be done well in advance of the party.

Brandy sour

45 ml/3 tbsp brandy

Juice of ½ lemon

Ice cubes

Sparkling mineral water

1 slice of lemon, for garnishing

1 Put the brandy and lemon juice in a shaker full of ice. Shake well, then pour into a tall glass.

2 Top up with sparkling water to taste, stir and serve garnished with a slice of lemon.

Whisky sour

60 ml/4 tbsp Scotch whisky

15 ml/1 tbsp pure orange juice

15 ml/1 tbsp lemon juice

7.5 ml/1½ tsp caster (superfine) sugar

1 Maraschino cherry, for garnishing

1 Mix all the ingredients together.

2 Pour into a cocktail glass and serve garnished with the Maraschino cherry.

Bloody Mary

150 ml/¼ pt/⅔ cup tomato juice

A good squeeze of lemon juice

A generous dash of Worcestershire sauce

A few drops of Tabasco sauce

30 ml/2 tbsp vodka

A pinch of salt

Crushed ice

1 small celery stick or slice of lemon, for garnishing

1 Put all the ingredients in a cocktail shaker or jug. Shake well or stir thoroughly, then strain into a heavy-based tumbler.

2 Add a celery stick to the drink or suspend a slice of lemon on the side of the glass and serve.

Fruit garnishes To decorate the side of a glass, cut a fairly thin slice of lemon, lime, small orange or cucumber (as appropriate). Make a cut from the centre to the edge of the slice. Gently open the cut and suspend the slice over the rim of the glass.

Manhattan

45 ml/3 tbsp Bourbon or Scotch whisky

15 ml/1 tbsp sweet red vermouth

A few drops of Angostura bitters

Cracked ice

1 Maraschino cherry, for garnishing (optional)

1 Mix the whisky and vermouth together in a heavy-based tumbler and add cracked ice.

2 Garnish with a cherry, if liked.

Martini

45 ml/3 tbsp gin

45 ml/3 tbsp dry vermouth

1 green olive or a twist of lemon peel,
for garnishing

1 Mix the gin and vermouth together in a cocktail glass.

2 Add an olive or twist of lemon peel. If serving Martini on the rocks, add crushed ice (although to purists, that's sacrilege).

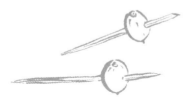

Gibson

Prepare as for a Martini (see above) but add a white cocktail (pearl) onion to each glass instead of the olive or lemon peel. Serve in a frosted glass.

Frosted glasses Fill the glasses with crushed ice and place in the fridge or freezer so that a cold mist forms on the outside when you use them.

Sidecar

60 ml/4 tbsp brandy

30 ml/2 tbsp Cointreau

1 small lemon

Cracked ice

1 Mix the brandy with the Cointreau in a jug.

2 Pare off a strip of lemon zest and reserve. Cut the fruit in half, squeeze the juice and pour through a sieve (strainer) into the alcohol.

3 Fill a tall tumbler with cracked ice. Add the strip of lemon zest. Pour in the alcohol and lemon mixture, stir with a swizzle stick and serve.

Rusty nail

Cracked ice

45 ml/3 tbsp Scotch whisky

15 ml/1 tbsp Drambuie

Ice cubes

1 Put lots of cracked ice in a cocktail shaker or jug.

2 Add the whisky and Drambuie and shake or stir well.

3 Fill a narrow tumbler with ice cubes. Strain the cocktail into the glass and serve.

Blueberry banger

30 ml/2 tbsp fresh blueberries

30 ml/2 tbsp ruby port

30 ml/2 tbsp vodka

30 ml/2 tbsp double (heavy) cream

A little cracked ice

1 Put all the ingredients in a blender and liquidise until smooth.

2 Strain the cocktail into a cocktail glass and serve straight away.

Mango Malibu

½ small mango, peeled and chopped

15 ml/1 tbsp icing (confectioners') sugar

Juice of 1 lime

60 ml/4 tbsp Malibu

Ice cubes

Sparkling mineral water

1 Put the mango in a blender with the sugar, lime and Malibu. Liquidise until smooth.

2 Fill a tall glass with ice cubes. Strain the mixture into the glass and top up with sparkling mineral water to taste. Stir with a swizzle stick and serve.

Edible swizzle sticks For any cold cocktails, add a stick of barley sugar to the glass for stirring the contents.

Strawberry sparkler

5 ml/1 tsp caster (superfine) sugar

30 ml/2 tbsp brandy

4–6 very small strawberries

Chilled sparkling white wine

1 Mix the sugar with the brandy in a large wine goblet until dissolved.

2 Add the strawberries, stir and, if possible, leave in the fridge to macerate for 30 minutes.

3 When ready to serve, top up with chilled sparkling white wine, stir once more and serve.

If you can get hold of wild strawberries, the cocktail tastes even better!

Sangria

SERVES 6–8

300 ml/½ pt/1¼ cups water

45 ml/3 tbsp caster (superfine) sugar

1 bottle of red wine

30 ml/2 tbsp lemon juice

1 orange, sliced

1 lemon, sliced

30 ml/2 tbsp brandy

300 ml/½ pt/1¼ cups lemonade, chilled

1 Mix all the ingredients except the lemonade in a large jug. Chill.

2 When ready to serve, add the lemonade, stir and pour.

You can increase the amount of lemonade to make this less potent, and leave out the brandy altogether, if you prefer.

Pimms

SERVES 6

5 cm/2 in piece of cucumber, thinly sliced

A handful of fresh borage or mint leaves

1 lemon, halved and sliced

½ bottle Pimms No 1 Cup

Ice cubes

Lemonade

1 Put the cucumber, borage or mint and lemon in a large jug and add the Pimms. Chill until ready to serve.

2 When ready to serve, top up the jug with lemonade to taste, stir and pour over ice in tall glasses.

Sunset

Cracked ice

30 ml/2 tbsp grenadine syrup

150 ml/¹⁄₄ pt/²⁄₃ cup pure orange juice

1 Half-fill a tall glass with cracked ice and add the grenadine syrup.

2 Tilt the glass and slowly pour in the orange juice so that most of it floats on top of the syrup. Do not mix.

Raspberry reveller

30 ml/2 tbsp crushed ice

30 ml/2 tbsp fresh raspberries

15 ml/1 tbsp raspberry cordial

10 ml/2 tsp lemon juice

150 ml/¹⁄₄ pt/²⁄₃ cup sparkling apple juice

1 Put the crushed ice in a large wine goblet. Add the raspberries, cordial and lemon juice. Stir lightly with a swizzle stick.

2 Top up with the sparkling apple juice, stir again and serve.

Melon frappé

1 wedge of ripe melon (any type), skinned and seeded

Juice of ¹⁄₂ lime

15 ml/1 tbsp icing (confectioners') sugar

Crushed ice

150 ml/¹⁄₄ pt/²⁄₃ cup ginger ale

1 Put the melon in a blender with the lime and icing sugar. Blend until smooth.

2 Half-fill a tall glass with crushed ice. Pour in the melon mixture.

3 Top with ginger ale, stir with a swizzle stick, and serve straight away.

Gaelic coffee

5 ml/1 tsp light brown sugar

30 ml/2 tbsp Scotch whisky

About 90 ml/6 tbsp hot black coffee

About 45 ml/3 tbsp double (heavy) cream, chilled

1 Spoon the sugar into a large wine goblet or small glass mug and add the whisky. Stir until dissolved.

2 Put a spoon in the glass, then pour on hot coffee, up to about 2 cm/³⁄₄ in from the top. Stir again and remove the spoon.

3 Hold a cold teaspoon, rounded side up, just touching the surface of the coffee, and slowly pour cream over the spoon to form a layer about 1 cm/¹⁄₂ in thick, floating on the top. Serve immediately.

Calypso coffee

Prepare as for Gaelic Coffee (above) but use dark rum instead of Scotch whisky.

Caribbean coffee

Prepare as for Gaelic Coffee (above) but use white rum instead of Scotch whisky.

French coffee

Prepare as for Gaelic Coffee (above) but use Cognac instead of Scotch whisky.

Italian coffee

Prepare as for Gaelic Coffee (above) but use Amaretto liqueur instead of Scotch whisky.

Mocha liqueur coffee

Prepare as for Gaelic Coffee (above) but use chocolate liqueur instead of Scotch whisky.

Russian coffee

Prepare as for Gaelic Coffee (above) but use vodka instead of Scotch whisky.

Brazilian mocha

25 g/1 oz/¼ cup plain (semi-sweet) chocolate, chopped

100 ml/3½ fl oz /scant ½ cup strong black coffee

5 ml/1 tsp demerara sugar

45 ml/3 tbsp double (heavy) cream

1 Put the chocolate and coffee in a saucepan and heat gently, stirring all the time, until the chocolate melts. Stir in the sugar and bring just to the boil.

2 Put a cold teaspoon in a large wine goblet. Pour in the hot chocolate and coffee.

3 Hold a cold teaspoon over the liquid, rounded side up, just touching the surface. Slowly pour over the cream so that it floats on the top. Serve straight away.

Hot coffees and chocolate Add a cinnamon stick to hot coffee or chocolate drinks for decoration or lay a mint chocolate stick beside the drink on the saucer, for the guest to stir and eat when ready.

Chocolate rumba

25 g/1 oz/¼ cup grated bitter dark chocolate

10 ml/2 tsp clear honey

175 ml/6 fl oz/¾ cup milk

30 ml/2 tbsp dark rum

30 ml/2 tbsp sweetened whipped double (heavy) cream, or cream from an aerosol can

A little ground cinnamon, for dusting

1 Put the grated chocolate into a saucepan with the honey and milk.

2 Heat gently, stirring all the time, until the chocolate has melted. Bring just to the boil.

3 Stir in the rum, then pour into a glass mug. Top with whipped cream, either piped or spooned, or squirt cream from an aerosol in a swirl over the top. Dust with cinnamon. Serve straight away.

Index

INDEX